Preface

The Commission has already surveyed the papers of nineteenth-century cabinet ministers and diplomats in its series of guides to sources for British history.[1] This volume sets out to describe the surviving papers of British colonial governors and senior officials of the Colonial Office and its predecessor departments in the same period between 1782 and 1900.[2]

The survey covers those colonies administered by the Colonial Office throughout the century or from their acquisition during it, those like the Falkland Islands and Straits Settlements formerly the responsibility of the Admiralty, the Foreign Office or the India Office and transferred to the Colonial Office before 1900, and those originally established by companies in Africa, South East Asia and North America, for which the British government later assumed responsibility. It does not, however, include British India and its dependencies, or the individual British North American provinces after each had joined the Dominion of Canada between 1867 and 1873.

For the purpose of the guide a colonial governor has been defined as the Crown's, or where appropriate the company's, representative at the head of the administration of a colony or group of colonies. The term includes governors-general, governors-in-chief, governors, lieutenant-governors, high commissioners and resident commissioners, as well as individuals temporarily administering a colony in the governor's absence. The guide also notices the papers of the secretaries of state in London with central responsibility for colonial affairs, together with their under secretaries and assistant under secretaries.

Altogether, some 1,200 individuals were identified for consideration,[3] of whom 353 were found to have left papers relevant to colonial affairs within the period. Best represented are the governors of the British North American provinces, Cape Colony and New South Wales, three-quarters of whom left papers described in the guide. By contrast there is a poorer survival rate for the papers of governors in Asia, Central and West Africa, and the West Indies, where in many cases a rapid succession of governors, and in some the relative unimportance of the posts, provided little opportunity or need for the accumulation of papers on a large scale.

The papers dealt with here are mainly those retained by an individual after leaving office and exclude the despatches and other official papers which form part of the Colonial Office records now held in the Public Record Office. Despatches exchanged between London and the colonies were open to the scrutiny of parliament and colonial governing councils. To ensure confidentiality secretaries of state and governors made use of private letters which remained the property of the recipient on giving up his post. These letters, which can be 'startlingly unlike' the despatches they are supposed to complement,[4] and the private correspondence that passed between governors themselves are probably the most historically significant of the papers described below. The other papers commonly retained included drafts and copies of official despatches, memoranda, reports and similar papers bearing on the internal administration of a colony, as well as more personal material such as diaries and reminiscences.

The guide contains summaries of 711 groups of papers. The great bulk is now to be found in public institutions throughout the world, 327 groups in 74 British libraries and record offices, and 292 groups in 80 institutions overseas. A further 76 groups remain in private hands, and the present location of 15 has not yet been established.

The Commission gratefully acknowledges the help it has received from the many owners and custodians who have made their collections available to its staff or responded generously to requests for information, and wishes particularly to express its gratitude to the institutions in the Commonwealth and elsewhere overseas which have supplied the National Register of Archives with much significant new information during the preparation of the guide. The research and editing of the guide have been carried out by Dr JG Parker, Dr SG Roberts and Mr RJ Sargent under the direction of Miss Sonia P Anderson and Dr CJ Kitching.

BS SMITH
Secretary
25 March 1986

Quality House, Quality Court,
Chancery Lane, London WC2A 1HP

---

[1] *Papers of British cabinet ministers 1782-1900* (HMSO, 1982), and *Private papers of British diplomats 1782-1900* (HMSO, 1985). Where papers have already been more fully described in these volumes, only material relating to colonial affairs has been included in this guide, with cross-references given to the fuller entries in the form 'See also *Cabinet Ministers*' and 'See also *Diplomats*'.

[2] Following the demise of the Board of Trade and the American secretaryship in 1782, the departments responsible for colonial affairs were successively the Home Office (1782-1801), the War and Colonial Office (1801-1854) and the Colonial Office (from 1854).

[3] DP Henige, *Colonial governors from the fifteenth century to the present* (Wisconsin, 1970); Joseph Haydn, *Book of dignities* (London, 1894; reprinted 1969); JC Sainty, *Colonial Office officials 1794-1870* (University of London Institute of Historical Research, 1976); *Colonial Office List*. In general the biographical details at the head of each entry in the guide note only the senior colonial posts held, with the outside and therefore sometimes overlapping dates of appointments or those of taking up or leaving office.

[4] RB Pugh, *The records of the Colonial and Dominions Offices* (HMSO, 1964), p50.

The Royal Commission on Historical Manuscripts

Guides to Sources for British History
based on the National Register of Archives

5

Private Papers of
BRITISH COLONIAL
GOVERNORS
1782 – 1900

London   Her Majesty's Stationery Office

HMSO publications are available from:

HMSO Publications Centre
(Mail and telephone orders only)
PO Box 276, London SW8 5DT
Telephone orders 01-622 3316
General enquiries 01-211 5656
(queuing system in operation for both numbers)

HMSO Bookshops
49 High Holborn, London, WC1V 6HB 01-211 5656 (Counter service only)
258 Broad Street, Birmingham, B1 2HE 021-643 3757
Southey House, 33 Wine Street, Bristol, BS1 2BQ (0272) 24306/24307
9-21 Princess Street, Manchester, M60 8AS 061-834 7201
80 Chichester Street, Belfast BT1 4JY (0232) 238451
13a Castle Street, Edinburgh, EH2 3AR 031-225 6333

HMSO's Accredited Agents
(see Yellow Pages)

and through good booksellers

Contents

Access to privately owned papers

Privately owned collections of papers that have been deposited on loan by their owners in libraries, record offices and other public institutions are normally available for research without restriction. Special conditions, however, may sometimes apply to their use, particularly if they are to be cited in published works. All enquiries on this point should be addressed to the institutions concerned.

Permission to see other privately owned collections should, in the first instance, be sought from their owners in writing. Applicants are reminded that such papers can normally be made available for use only at considerable personal inconvenience and expense to their owners, and that access for purposes of research is a privilege, not a right. The conditions of access to individual collections were those prevailing in March 1986. Enquiries about papers described simply as in private or family possession should be addressed to the Commission.

Unpublished lists of which copies may be consulted in the National Register of Archives are cited by their number there, eg NRA 28356.

Private papers of British colonial governors 1782-1900

[1] ABERCROMBY, Lieutenant-General Sir Ralph (1734-1801)
Acting governor of Trinidad 1797.

Orderly book, W Indies 1797.
National Army Museum (7712-43). Purchased at Sotheby's 5 Dec 1977, lot 427. Correspondence with Henry Dundas, William Huskisson and others, used in *Lieutenant-General Sir Ralph Abercromby KB 1793-1801: a memoir by his son James Lord Dunfermline* (1861), has not been traced.

ABERDEEN, Earls of, see Gordon; Hamilton-Gordon G.

ABERDEEN AND TEMAIR, Marquess of, see Gordon.

[2] ACHESON, Archibald (1776-1849), styled Lord Acheson 1806-7, 2nd Earl of Gosford 1807
Governor-in-chief of British North America 1835-8.

Official and private corresp with Lord Glenelg 1835-8 (2 vols, 23 bundles); letters from the lieutenant-governors in British N America 1835-8 (202 items); letters of introduction and patronage 1835-9 (79 items); misc corresp 1835-40 (125 items); misc papers 1824, 1834-7 (16 items).
Public Record Office of Northern Ireland (D2259). Deposited by the 7th Earl of Gosford. NRA 28356.

[3] ADAM, General Sir Frederick (1781-1853)
High commissioner for the Ionian Islands 1824-32.

Letters mainly from James Loch 1801-30 (44 items); misc corresp and papers 1800-53, mainly rel to his marriages 1811 and 1820, the Peninsular war 1812-13, and his appointment as high commissioner 1824 (c50 items); letters from him to his father, his brothers and his first wife c1794-1838 (2 boxes, c480 items).
RK Adam Esq. Enquiries to NRA (Scotland). NRA 9954.

[4] AIREY, General Richard (1803-1881), Baron Airey 1876
Governor of Gibraltar 1865-70.

Letters from his brother James 1834-44 (24 items), his uncle Thomas Talbot 1840-50 (46 items), Lord Hardinge 1854-5 (101 items), and the Duke of Cambridge c1858-1865 (108 items); corresp and papers mainly rel to his financial affairs and his estate at Port Talbot, Upper Canada 1827-66 (1 vol, c190 items); letter book, Toronto 1838-9 and diary, Port Talbot 1850-1 (1 vol); scrapbook 1840-60 (1 vol); Gibraltar Palace guest lists and menus 1875-8 (1 vol).
Hereford RO (G/IV/A, E47, E47A). Deposited by his great-grandson Sir RCG Cotterell Bt 1963-4. NRA 10872.

Letters to him from various correspondents and from him to his solicitor HCF Becher rel to the Port Talbot estate c1848-c1869 (c200 items).
University of Western Ontario Library, London (CA9 ON AIR 001). Presented by descendants of HCF Becher c1940.

[5] ALEXANDER, Du Pré (1777-1839), styled Viscount Alexander 1800-2, 2nd Earl of Caledon 1802
Governor of Cape Colony 1806-11.

Copies of despatches to and from him 1806-11 (7 vols), of unofficial letters from him mainly 1806-12 (2 vols, 26 items), of his reports to Lord Minto 1807-11 (1 vol), and of official letters from the colonial secretary at the Cape 1807-11 (6 vols); official diaries 1807-11 (5 vols); schedules of papers laid before him 1807-11 (8 vols); papers rel to the judiciary 1802-11 (39 vols and bundles, 50 items); letters from Colonel Robert Collins, and journal of Collins's expedition to the interior, 1808-9 (3 vols); commission, instructions and misc papers rel to Cape Colony 1795-1811 (6 vols, etc); maps, plans and drawings, S Africa and Indian Ocean 1796-c1810 (c40 items); proclamations and other printed material 1807-11 (13 vols); corresp and papers rel to Cape Colony mainly after his departure, 1809-30 (190 items); corresp and papers rel to local politics

and defence in co Tyrone, the Irish representative peerage, the borough of Old Sarum, etc 1798-1839 (2 vols, *c*510 items); family and business corresp and papers 1804-39 (*c*400 items).
Public Record Office of Northern Ireland (D2431, D2433). Deposited by the Trustees of the Caledon Estates 1969. NRA 13276.

[6] **ALLEYNE, John Foster** (1762-1823)
Administrator of Barbados 1817.

Copies of letters from him, mainly rel to business and estate affairs, Barbados and England 1799-1804 (1 vol).
University of the West Indies Library, St Augustine, Trinidad. Purchased by the government of Trinidad from the W India Committee 1981. JS Handler, *Guide to source materials for Barbados history 1627-1834*, Carbondale and Edwardsville, Illinois 1971, p159; NRA 25250.

Copies of corresp with merchants and others 1811-14 (1 vol).
Bodleian Library, Oxford (MS Eng. misc. e. 245). Presented by the Oxford Book Salvage Campaign 1943.

[7] **ANTROBUS, Sir Reginald Laurence** (1853-1942)
Acting governor of St Helena 1889-90; assistant under secretary for the colonies 1898-1909.

Corresp with Lord Knutsford and others rel to the exile of Dinuzulu on St Helena 1890-7 (18 items).
Rhodes House Library, Oxford (MSS Afr. s.223). Presented by Miss EG Antrobus 1960.

ARGYLL, Duke of, see Campbell JDS.

[8] **ARTHUR, Lieutenant-General Sir George** (1784-1854), 1st Bt 1841
Superintendent of British Honduras 1814-22; lieutenant-governor of Van Diemen's Land 1824-36, of Upper Canada 1837-41.

Drafts and copies of despatches and letters to Lord Bathurst, the Duke of Manchester and Lord Palmerston, army officers and magistrates in British Honduras, etc 1814-22 (15 vols); proclamation book 1814-22, and warrant books 1815-22 (4 vols); corresp and papers rel to the cases of Major Bradley, Major Lord and Gunner Ingram 1820-4, 1837 (18 files); misc corresp and papers, British Honduras mainly 1810-24 (12 files); personal financial papers 1809-32 (9 vols and files).
Royal Commonwealth Society. Purchased from Miss LF Arthur 1956. NRA 6388.

Letters from Sir Richard Bourke, Sir TM Brisbane, Sir Ralph Darling, Alfred Stephen and others in Australia 1823-45 (17 vols); corresp with Sir James Stephen and the Colonial Office 1823-54, with index 1823-35 (4 vols); general corresp 1821-50 (12 vols); corresp and papers, Van Diemen's Land

1811-55, mainly 1824-36, rel to aborigines, convicts, land grants, legal cases, the settlement of Port Phillip, etc (31 vols).
Mitchell Library, Sydney (A 2161-2220, D 290-2). Purchased from the Society for the Propagation of the Gospel 1936.

Corresp and papers, Van Diemen's Land 1825-52, incl corresp rel to his salary 1825-6, legal papers and accounts rel to his property 1841-52, and his answers to questions on the convict system (1 box).
Mitchell Library, Sydney (Uncat MS Set 359). Purchased from Miss LF Arthur 1956.

Letters from British statesmen, British N American governors and politicians and others, with a few draft replies and related papers, Upper Canada 1837-42 (1,232 items); copies of letters from him *c*1837-41 (6 vols); letters to him as governor of Bombay 1842-6 (800 items); copies of letters from him 1842-51 (9 vols).
Metropolitan Toronto Library. Purchased 1938, 1941-4, 1956.

AYLMER, Baron, see Whitworth-Aylmer.

[9] **BAGOT, Sir Charles** (1781-1843)
Governor-in-chief of British North America 1841-3.

Letters, petitions and addresses to him, mainly as governor-in-chief, 1838-42 (5 vols).
Public Archives of Canada, Ottawa (MG24 A13, vols 2-6). Presented by JF Bagot 1910.

Corresp rel to British N America while minister to the United States 1816-19 (1 vol); corresp and papers as governor-in-chief *c*1840-3, incl letters of recommendation to him, copies of his despatches and private letters to Lord Stanley, and printed Cabinet papers rel to colonial defence (1 box).
OR Bagot Esq. Enquiries to Cumbria RO, Kendal. NRA 6234. Transcripts are in the Public Archives of Canada (MG24 A13, vols 1, 7-14).

See also *Diplomats.*

[10] **BAIRD, General Sir David** (1757-1829), 1st Bt 1809
Acting governor of Cape Colony 1806-7.

Selected corresp and papers 1772-1828, incl letters from Lord Castlereagh and Sir HR Popham and other items rel to Cape Colony 1805-7 (4 vols); letter book, Cape Colony, incl copies of letters to Castlereagh, Robert Patton, Popham and William Windham 1805-7 (1 vol); military letter books 1791-7, 1801-2 (7 vols); letters from him to Lieutenant-Colonel Keith Young 1798-1809 (30 items); corresp with the Treasury, etc rel to sums allowed to officers on the Cape expeditions, prize money for the Buenos Aires campaign and expenditure in Spain, 1801-13 (68 items); military account books 1800-3, 1809-20 (3 vols); misc corresp and papers 1796-1829, incl corresp with Popham and Windham 1806-7, letters rel to Spain 1808-9 and record of service to 1809 (48 items).

Scottish United Services Museum. Deposited by Sir DC Baird Bt 1948. NRA 27982.

Military and financial letter book 1804-13.
National Library of Scotland (MS 6108). Presented by Sir WS Haldane and Mrs Campbell Fraser 1945.

Official corresp while serving in Spain 1808-9 (52ff).
British Library (Add MS 43224 ff278-329). Presented 1932 among the papers of his nephew Sir Alexander Gordon by the 1st Marquess of Aberdeen.

BALCARRES, Earl of, see Lindsay.

[11] **BALFOUR, Blayney Townley** (1799-1882)
Lieutenant-governor of the Bahamas 1833-5.

Corresp and papers, Bahamas 1832-4 (50 items); address to him on his departure 1835 (1 item); passports 1849, 1862 (2 items); personal accounts 1866-74 (1 vol).
National Library of Ireland (MSS 10253-4, 10358, 11906). Deposited 1955 by David Crichton, sometime owner of Townley Hall, the Balfour seat.
Manuscript sources for the history of Irish civilisation, ed RJ Hayes, iv, Boston 1965, pp658-63.

Corresp of Lord Goderich 1832, incl letters from various correspondents to Balfour as his private secretary (3 vols).
British Library (Add MSS 40878-80). Presented by the executors of the 2nd Marquess of Ripon 1923.

[12] **BALL, Rear-Admiral Sir Alexander John** (1757-1809), 1st Bt 1801
Civil commissioner for Malta 1799-1801, 1802-9.

Diary 1799-1800 and misc papers, Malta 1798-1808, incl notes on its history and institutions, and memorandum on revenues.
Untraced. Sold at Sotheby's 14 Oct 1974, lot 561.

[13] **BANNERMAN, James** (1790-1858)
Lieutenant-governor of the Gold Coast 1850-1.

Letters from Brodie Cruickshank, SJ Hill and others, and misc papers, 1824, 1842-54 (25 items).
National Archives of Ghana, Accra (Special Collection 2). NRA 28613.

[14] **BARKER, Collet** (1786-1831)
Commandant at Raffles Bay 1828-9.

Journals, Raffles Bay 1828-9 and King George's Sound 1830-1 (2 vols).
Archives Office of New South Wales, Sydney (9/2747-8). Transferred from the Mitchell Library, Sydney, which received them in 1934 from the New South Wales chief secretary's department.

[15] **BARKLY, Sir Henry** (1815-1898)
Governor of British Guiana 1848-53, of Jamaica 1853-6, of Victoria 1856-63, of Mauritius 1863-70, of Cape Colony 1870-7.

Corresp, notes and memoranda, incl letters from Edward Cardwell, JA Froude, the 5th Duke of Newcastle and others *c*1843-76 (*c*50 items).
Mrs M Macmillan (his great-great niece).
M Macmillan, *Sir Henry Barkly, mediator and moderator, 1815-1898,* Cape Town 1970.

Misc letters received rel to his colonial career and public life in England 1849-94 (*c*50 items).
Westminster City Libraries, Marylebone Local History Library. Presented *c*1943 by his grandson-in-law Douglas Timins. NRA 28107.

Papers rel to *Stapeliae* 1873-7.
Royal Botanic Gardens, Kew.

[16] **BARLEE, Sir Frederick Palgrave** (1827-1884)
Lieutenant-governor of British Honduras 1877-83, of Trinidad 1884.

Letters to his brother William 1876-84 (109 items); personal accounts 1884 (1 vol).
Mrs MC Barlee. A microfilm is in the National Library of Australia, Canberra (M594).

[17] **BARNES, Lieutenant-General Sir Edward** (1776-1838)
Lieutenant-governor of Ceylon 1820-1, governor 1824-31.

Register of despatches to Lord Bathurst 1820-6 (2 vols).
British Library (Add MSS 19454-5). Purchased at Sotheby's 9 Apr 1853, lot 882.

[18] **BARRY, Sir Redmond** (1813-1880)
Administrator of Victoria 1875.

Corresp with his family, friends, British and Australian politicians and others, rel to family and financial affairs, politics in Victoria, the development of Melbourne University and the Public Library of Victoria, etc 1829-80 (*c*550 items); letters to his mother 1862-3 (1 vol); journal, Rome 1862 (2 vols); day books 1837-72 (133ff); accounts and receipts 1862-79 (7 vols, *c*60 items); misc papers incl legal notes, literary MSS, commissions, addresses and inventories 1837-77 (5 vols, *c*35 bundles and items).
La Trobe Library, Melbourne (MS 8380). Presented by Mrs Sheila O'Sullivan 1954-5. NRA 25513.

Visitors' book 1875.
National Library of Australia, Canberra (MS 3223). Presented by Sir JA Ferguson 1969.

[19] **BATHURST, Henry** (1762-1834), styled Lord Apsley 1775-94, 3rd Earl Bathurst 1794 Secretary of state for war and the colonies 1812-27.

Despatches, etc rel to Cape Colony and to the slave trade 1815-26 (2 vols); official and private corresp with Sir Frederick Adam, Sir Thomas Maitland and others, Ionian Islands and Malta 1816-23 (18 vols); private corresp with Sir Hudson Lowe, St Helena 1816-25 (7 vols); letters from correspondents in the colonies 1824 (3 vols); general corresp 1812-27 (16 vols); letters from him to his private secretary 1825-8 (3 vols); copies of private letters from him rel to colonial affairs 1821-7 (4 vols); copy of the memoirs of Count de las Cases 1815-16 and Sir Pulteney Malcolm's notes of interviews with Napoleon 1816 (5 vols).
British Library (MS Loan 57). Deposited by the 8th Earl Bathurst 1965. NRA 20952.

See also *Cabinet Ministers*.

BEAUCHAMP, Earl, see Lygon.

[20] **BELL, Sir Henry Hesketh Joudou** (1864-1952)
Administrator of Dominica 1899-1905; commissioner for Uganda 1905-7; governor of Uganda 1907-9, of Northern Nigeria 1909-12, of the Leeward Islands 1912-15, of Mauritius 1915-24.

Letters from him mainly to his aunt (1 bundle); subject files mainly rel to his literary interests (c10 files); notebooks 1889-96 and nd (6 vols); synopses of his diaries 1890-1940 (5 vols); scrapbooks of invitations, photographs, press cuttings, etc 1889-1924 (6 vols); albums of water-colours and photographs, and misc papers 1906-c1927 and nd.
Royal Commonwealth Society. Bequeathed by him to Mrs AR Llewellin-Taylour, and presented on her death in 1968. Access to some of the papers is restricted. *Manuscript catalogue*, pp38-9.

Diaries c1890-c1940.
British Library. Bequeathed by him on condition that access should be withheld for fifty years after his death.

BELMORE, Earls, see Lowry-Corry.

[21] **BERNARD** (afterwards **BERNARD MORLAND**), **Sir Scrope** (1758-1830), 4th Bt 1818
Non-permanent under secretary for home affairs 1789-92.

Corresp with Lord Buckingham, Henry Dundas, Lord Grenville, Evan Nepean and others, mainly 1789-92 (c340 items); corresp 1789-92 arranged by subject, incl Bay of Honduras, Quebec and transportation of convicts (20 files); returns mainly of militia officers 1790-1 (51 items); corresp rel to Ireland 1782-c1830, mainly as private secretary to the lord lieutenant 1782-3, 1787-9 (c420 items);

corresp and papers rel to parliamentary elections and to Buckinghamshire local defence and administration 1775-1830 (c325 items); corresp with clients as a banker and as an advocate in Doctors' Commons 1780-1830 (c330 items); personal and family corresp 1775-c1830 (c550 items).
Buckinghamshire RO (D/SB). Deposited by Mrs EP Spencer Bernard 1980. NRA 7343.

[22] **BIDDULPH, General Sir Robert** (1835-1918)
High commissioner for Cyprus 1879-86; governor of Gibraltar 1893-1900.

Corresp, reports and orders in council, Cyprus 1878-89 (10 vols); papers rel to the China war 1860 (1 vol); misc corresp and papers 1850-1920 (1 vol); commissions and warrants 1850-99 (3 vols).
Royal Artillery Institution (MD/1120). Deposited by the Ministry of Defence 1980. Access by prior written application. NRA 25822.

[23] **BIRCH, Sir Ernest Woodford** (1857-1929)
Resident in Selangor 1892-7, in Negri Sembilan 1897-1900; governor of Labuan and North Borneo 1901-4; resident in Perak 1904-10.

Letters to him from Colonial Office officials, administrators in the Malay states, friends and others 1889-1929 (2 bundles); draft autobiography, other writings rel to his career and travel accounts, Malayan peninsula 1883, 1920-1, and misc papers 1852-1927 (7 bundles).
Rhodes House Library, Oxford (MSS Ind. Ocn.s.242/2-3). NRA 17771.

[24] **BIRCH, James Wheeler Woodford** (1826-1875)
Resident in Perak 1874-5.

Diaries, Perak 1874-5 (3 vols); corresp and press cuttings rel to his murder there 1875 (1 vol).
Rhodes House Library, Oxford (MSS Ind. Ocn. s. 242/1). NRA 17771.

[25] **BISHOP, William** (fl 1793-1801)
Administrator of Barbados 1793-4, 1800-1.

Copies of his corresp and of addresses from the legislative assembly 1800-1, with a few original letters to him from governors of French W Indian islands (1 vol).
Scottish Record Office (GD 46/7/1). Presented among the papers of Lord Seaforth by Mr and Mrs FA Stewart-Mackenzie 1954.

[26] **BLIGH, Vice-Admiral William** (1754-1817)
Governor of New South Wales 1805-9.

Corresp of him and members of his family 1789-1813 (1 vol); copies of his letters and despatches 1808-10 (1 vol); logs of HMS *Bounty* 1787-8, 1789-90 (2 vols); fair copy of log of *Bounty*'s launch,

Tonga to Timor 1789, with charts (1 vol); index to
Bounty's log, Tahiti 1788-9 (1 vol); his statement of
events on the *Bounty* voyage 1787-9, and misc
papers rel to the mutiny 1789; logs of HMS
Providence 1791-3 (2 vols); fragment of journal,
Cape of Good Hope 1791; drawings of fauna 1791-
3 (1 vol); papers rel to battles of Camperdown 1797
and Copenhagen 1801; misc papers incl
commissions 1790-1804 and draft memorial to Lord
Bathurst 1813; annotated copies of proceedings of
courts martial of *Bounty* mutineers 1792 and of
Colonel George Johnston 1811 (2 vols).
Mitchell Library, Sydney (S1/34-7, 43-8; A 564;
C 1013; DOC 556; PXA 565). The bulk of the
collection was presented by WR Bligh 1902, the
remainder acquired from various sources at later
dates. NRA 25523.

Private log giving *Bounty*'s course from England to
the Pacific 1787-9, written on printed instructions
for astronomical observations (1 vol); charts and
sketches made by him 1789-93 (1 vol).
Dixson Library, Sydney (MS 186; Bligh Charts Safe
item). Purchased by Sir William Dixson 1914, and
bequeathed by him 1952.

Corrected copy of log of *Providence* 1791-3 (2 vols).
Oxley Memorial Library, Brisbane (OM 71-34).

Notebook kept during voyage of *Bounty*'s launch
1789.
National Library of Australia, Canberra (MS 5393).
Purchased at Christie's 24 Nov 1976, lot 242.

[27] **BOURKE, General Sir Richard**
(1777-1855)
Lieutenant-governor of the Eastern Cape and acting
governor of Cape Colony 1825-8; governor of New
South Wales 1831-7.

Corresp and papers mainly rel to Cape Colony,
comprising letters to him 1825-9 (5 vols), drafts and
copies of letters from him 1826-45 (3 vols), indexes
to despatches received 1826-8 (2 vols), instructions
to him 1816-27 (2 vols) and to civil commissioners
1827-8 (2 vols), corresp and papers rel to frontier
wars and relations with the Zulus 1826 and nd
(3 vols), papers rel to finance, the judiciary, etc
1821-8 (14 vols).
Rhodes House Library, Oxford (MSS Afr. t.7).
Purchased from the Museum Book Store 1941.
NRA 26112.

Copies of letters from him 1812-14 (4 vols); draft
despatches 1833-7 (4 vols); corresp mainly with his
son Richard 1833-7 (3 vols); corresp with Lord
Monteagle of Brandon 1828-55 (1 vol); misc letters
received 1828-54, some rel to New South Wales
(2 vols); journal of his voyage to England 1838
(1 vol); addresses presented to him and misc papers
nd (4 vols).
Mitchell Library, Sydney (A 1728-42, D 184).
Purchased from the Museum Book Store 1938-9.

General corresp 1824-50 (4 vols); corresp rel to
Cape Colony 1825-38 (1 vol), to New South Wales,
etc 1830-49 (1 vol), and with Lord Monteagle and
others rel to Ireland 1820-50 (2 vols); reports on

convicts and crime, New South Wales and Van
Diemen's Land, etc 1831-8 (2 vols); corresp and
papers rel to publication of Edmund Burke's letters
1824-52 (1 vol).
Mitchell Library, Sydney (ML MSS 403/2-12).
Purchased from GP Bourke at Sotheby's 23 Feb
1953, lots 306-11, 313, 315, 317. NRA 25899.

Corresp and papers, Cape Colony 1828-40 (35
items) and New South Wales 1835-8; family and
Irish corresp and papers 18th-19th cent; travel
journal, Malta, France and Germany 1845-6.
Untraced. Sold at Sotheby's 23 Feb 1953, lot 312
and 22 June 1953, lots 129, 131-3.

Corresp with his son Richard, Lord Monteagle and
others 1820-54, and papers mainly rel to co
Limerick 1822-51 (*c*700 items).
National Library of Ireland (MSS 8474, 8476-8).
Purchased at Sotheby's 23 Feb 1953, lot 314 and
22 June 1953, lot 130.

Letters to his son Richard 1830-50, misc letters
received 1835-47, and papers rel to his estates in co
Limerick (2 vols).
Mitchell Library, Sydney (ML MSS 2328).
Presented by Miss Slaney Osborne 1972.

Letters from Sir George Arthur 1832-6 (42 items).
Mitchell Library, Sydney (A 1962). Purchased from
Maggs Bros Ltd 1934.

Diary of his visit to Melbourne, Geelong and
Mount Macedon 1837 (1 vol); letters from Captain
Lonsdale RN 1835-7 (6 items).
La Trobe Library, Melbourne (MSS 5176, 5182-7).
Purchased 1935.

[28] **BOWEN, Sir George Ferguson** (1821-1899)
Governor of Queensland 1859-67, of New Zealand
1867-73, of Victoria 1873-9, of Mauritius 1879-82,
of Hong Kong 1882-7.

Journal, Greece 1850 (1 vol); commissions, letters
to him and press cuttings 1841-93 (1 file).
Queensland Women's Historical Association, Brisbane.

Confidential report to Lord Lyttelton on the Maori
rebellion 1869 (1 vol).
Alexander Turnbull Library, Wellington (MS 1869).

Press cutting book 1868-78, annotated and indexed
by him.
Peter Newman Esq. NRA 27331. A microfilm is in
the National Library of Australia, Canberra
(M1920).

[29] **BOWER, Sir Graham John** (1848-1933)
Administrator of Mauritius 1900-1, 1903-4, 1906,
1908-9.

Corresp with secretaries and under secretaries of
state for the colonies, Sir HGR Robinson and other
colonial governors, S African statesmen, etc 1885-
1933, incl many letters rel to the Jameson raid and
his dismissal as imperial secretary to the high
commissioner 1896-7 (304 items); reminiscences of

his service in S Africa, press cuttings, etc 1894-
1933 (3 vols, 20 items).
South African Library, Cape Town (MSB 72).
Mainly bequeathed by him. NRA 28122.

Misc corresp 1897-8, 1926-32 (15 items); his
narrative written in 1900 of events leading to the
Jameson raid and the S African war (1 vol).
Rhodes House Library, Oxford (MSS Afr. s.63,
1279). Presented by his daughter 1969 and by Sir
BH Blackwell 1941.

[30] **BOWRING, Sir John** (1792-1872)
Governor of Hong Kong 1854-9.

Papers rel to his missions to China c1839-1857, incl
corresp with Sir George Balfour, Lords Clarendon
and Dalhousie, Sir GT Staunton, Sir James Stirling
and Sir HG Ward (623 items).
University of California Library, Los Angeles. See
National union catalog, MS 71-842.

Letters to him and papers 1822-64, mainly Hong
Kong 1854-9 (1 vol, 83 items); letters from his son
Frederick 1837-64 (65 items).
John Rylands University Library of Manchester
(English MSS 1229-30). Purchased at Christie's
8 Dec 1958, lot 286. *Hand-list of additions to the
collection of English manuscripts 1952-1970,* p26.

Corresp with statesmen, politicians and others
1816-65, incl letters to him in China and Hong
Kong from Lords Clarendon, Dalhousie and
Palmerston (119 items).
*Houghton Library, Harvard University, Cambridge,
Massachusetts* (b MS Eng 1247). Acquired 1966-71.
NRA 20033.

Letters to members of the Bowring family c1691-
c1910, mainly to him c1814-69, incl some rel to
Hong Kong (c250 items).
University College London (MS Ogden 62).
Purchased from CK Ogden 1953.

Letters to him and members of his family from
political, religious and literary figures 1795-1908
(176 items).
Huntington Library, San Marino, California.
Purchased 1967 from Francis Edwards Ltd, by
whom they had been acquired at Sotheby's 15 May
1967, lot 222. *National union catalog,* MS 71-1046.

Corresp and misc papers 1810-71 (c45 items).
Wellcome Historical Medical Library, London.
Purchased from Glendining & Co Ltd 29 Apr
1935, lot 334 and 27 May 1935, lot 419.

See also *Diplomats.*

[31] **BOYD, General Sir Robert** (1710-1794)
Lieutenant-governor of Gibraltar 1768-87, governor
1790-4.

Journal of his headquarters at Gibraltar 1781-3, incl
an account of the siege, and returns of the state of
the garrison, etc (2 vols).
British Library (Add MSS 38605-6). Purchased at
Sotheby's 26 July 1912, lot 1174.

Letter book as commissary general for Hessian
troops in Germany 1758.
National Army Museum (7908-34). Purchased at
Sotheby's 23 July 1979, lot 1.

[32] **BOYLE, David** (1833-1915), 7th Earl of
Glasgow 1890
Governor of New Zealand 1892-7.

Corresp with RJ Seddon 1894-5 (2 bundles); letters
from his factor in Ceylon 1903-6 (2 bundles); misc
addresses to him 1892-1908 (6 items); sketches and
photographs 1892-5, and press cuttings 1892-1901
(4 vols).
Rear-Admiral the Earl of Glasgow. Enquiries to
NRA (Scotland). NRA 10152 (pp31-2, 37-9).

BRABOURNE, Baron, see Knatchbull-Hugessen.

[33] **BRISBANE, Rear-Admiral Sir Charles**
(c1769-1829)
Governor of Curaçao 1807, of St Vincent 1808-29.

Misc papers c1780-c1829, incl a copy of his speech
to the legislature of St Vincent 1819, and duplicate
despatches and memorials, St Vincent nd (1 file);
copy of an address to George IV 1820.
Sir HSP Monro (his great-great-great-grandson).
Enquiries to NRA (Scotland). NRA 11854.

[34] **BRISBANE** (afterwards **MAKDOUGALL-
BRISBANE**), **General Sir Thomas** (1773-1860),
Bt 1836
Governor of New South Wales 1820-5.

Corresp 1812-37 and papers 1815-58, incl reports,
addresses to him 1825, and autobiographical notes
(4 boxes, c110 items).
National Library of Australia, Canberra (MS 4036).
Presented by Sir R de C Nan Kivell 1971.

Corresp 1802-59 and personal and misc papers
1792-1857 (1 vol); military papers 1792-1857,
mainly 1792-1815 (1 vol); family papers 1715-1870
(1 vol).
Mitchell Library, Sydney (ML MSS 1191).
Purchased 1965 from Winifred A Myers
(Autographs) Ltd.

Letters from astronomers and others 1818-49,
instructions 1821, religious notes 1823-5 and other
papers 1820-45 (1 box, 1 vol).
Mitchell Library, Sydney (ML MSS 419). Purchased
at Sotheby's 15 Dec 1958, lots 455-6, 460, 462, and
from Maggs Bros Ltd 1959.

Letter books 1822-5 (3 vols).
Mitchell Library, Sydney (A 1559). Acquired from A
Hart 1922.

Misc corresp rel to New South Wales 1819-26 (2
bundles).
CBH Scott Esq (a descendant of his wife's aunt
Anne Scott). Enquiries to NRA (Scotland). NRA
10544.

Corresp and accounts rel to estate, local and military business 1795-1858 (*c*220 items).
Mitchell Library, Glasgow (Brisbane Family Papers). NRA 24533.

Misc corresp and papers rel to astronomy *c*1807-49 (2 bundles).
Sir HSP Monro (great-great-great-grandson of his cousin Sir Charles Brisbane). Enquiries to NRA (Scotland). NRA 11854.

Diaries, Spain 1813 (2 vols).
DI Douglas-Wilson Esq.

Corresp, reports and memoranda, British N America 1813-15 (64 items).
William L Clements Library, University of Michigan, Ann Arbor. Purchased 1961.

[35] **BROCK, Major-General Sir Isaac**
(1769-1812)
Administrator of Upper Canada 1811-12.

Corresp and papers 1811-12, mainly letters from Sir George Prevost 1812, and misc papers of his nephew FB Tupper 1846 (1 vol).
Public Archives of Canada, Ottawa (MG24 A1). NRA 25948.

Diary as commander of the garrison at Quebec 1805.
Quebec Citadel Museum.

[36] **BROOKE, Sir James** (1803-1868)
Governor of Labuan 1847-56.

Letters mainly from his nephew JB Brooke 1849-66 (146 items); copies of corresp 1851-3 and press cuttings 1849-52 rel to Siam (1 vol); papers mainly rel to charges against him 1847-64 and negotiations rel to the future of Sarawak 1859-63, copies of letters to various correspondents 1852-62, and verses *c*1830-48 (*c*75 items).
Rhodes House Library, Oxford (MSS Pac. s.90). Presented by Vice-Admiral BCB Brooke 1975. NRA 21238.

[37] **BROWN, John** (d 1797)
Administrator of Barbados 1786-7.
Corresp of him and his family 1761-1835, mainly with relatives and merchants in Britain, N America and the W Indies 1761-99 (*c*140 items).
New York Historical Society (Misc MSS Brown, J).

[38] **BROWNE, Howe Peter** (1788-1845), styled Viscount Westport 1788-1800 and Earl of Altamont 1800-9, 2nd Marquess of Sligo 1809
Governor of Jamaica 1833-6.

Copies of despatches and private letters from him 1834-6 (7 vols); memorandum book *c*1834-6 (1 vol); papers rel to legal cases brought before him 1836 (1 vol); copies of misc letters and papers rel to his resignation 1835-6 (*c*40 items); addresses to him mainly on his resignation 1836-9 (21 items); letters to him rel to Jamaican affairs 1837-8 (15 items); papers rel to the Browne plantations in Jamaica 1735-1856 (*c*40 items).
Institute of Jamaica, Kingston (A34). Purchased from IK Fletcher after sale at Christie's 6 Oct 1958, lots 92-6, 120. KE Ingram, *Sources of Jamaican history 1655-1838*, i, 1976, pp315-21. Personal and family corresp in the sale (lots 88-91, 121) has not been traced.

Political, personal and family corresp 1815-39 (251 items).
Trinity College, Dublin (MS 6403). Purchased at Sotheby's 25 Mar 1974, lot 271. NRA 25244.

[39] **BROWNE, Colonel Sir Thomas Gore**
(1807-1887)
Governor of St Helena 1851-4, of New Zealand 1854-61, of Tasmania 1862-8; administrator of Bermuda 1870-1.

Letters from the Colonial Office 1855-61, governors of Australian colonies 1857-66, New Zealand politicians and missionaries, etc 1856-66 (257 items); copies of his despatches 1856-61 (2 vols); copies of his private letters and memoranda to colonial governors and others 1855-71 (2 vols); registers of general corresp 1866-72 (2 vols); letters to his family 1856-62 (2 vols); addresses to him, press cuttings and misc papers 1855-63 (1 box).
National Archives of New Zealand, Wellington (Gore Browne Papers). Presented by Sir Stewart Gore Browne 1952, except for a letter book transferred from the Alexander Turnbull Library 1968. NRA 1044.

Diaries 1857, 1861, 1863-4.
Mrs JS Harvey (his great-granddaughter).

[40] **BROWNRIGG, General Sir Robert**
(1759-1833), 1st Bt 1816
Governor of Ceylon 1811-20.

Copies of letters to the Duke of York as commander-in-chief 1795-1805 (2 vols); general letter books 1796-1811 (11 vols); despatches rel to military affairs in Ceylon 1818-20 (1 vol); military journal 1809 (1 vol); inspection reports on E India Co recruits 1792-8 (1 vol); notes on Zante and Martinique (1 vol).
Public Record Office (WO 133). Presented by Beatrice, Lady Brownrigg 1939.

[41] **BRUCE, James** (1811-1863), styled Lord Bruce 1840-1, 8th Earl of Elgin 1841
Governor of Jamaica 1842-6; governor-in-chief of British North America 1846-54.

Official and family corresp and papers, Jamaica 1842-6 (*c*2 boxes); draft despatches to the Colonial Office 1846-55 (1 bundle); drafts 1847-51 and copies 1847-9 of his private letters to Lord Grey (1 vol, 5 bundles); corresp and papers rel to commerce, communications, defence etc, British N America 1823-58, mainly 1846-54 (*c*5 bundles).

The Earl of Elgin. Access restricted. A microfilm of the N American papers is in the Public Archives of Canada, Ottawa (MG24 A16).

See also *Cabinet Ministers* and *Diplomats*.

BUCKINGHAM AND CHANDOS, Duke of, see Grenville RPC.

BUCKINGHAMSHIRE, Earl of, see Hobart.

BUCKLEY-MATHEW, see Mathew.

[42] **BULGER, Andrew** (1789-1858)
Governor of Assiniboia 1822-3.

Papers of him and his sons 1810-70, incl some rel to his service in the Royal Newfoundland Regiment 1810-15, and as governor of Assiniboia (7 vols).
Public Archives of Canada, Ottawa (MG19 E5). Presented by AE Bulger 1889.

[43] **BULWER, Sir Henry Ernest Gascoyne** (1836-1914)
Administrator of Dominica 1867-9; governor of Labuan 1871-5; lieutenant-governor of Natal 1875-80, governor 1882-5; high commissioner for Cyprus 1885-92.

Letter book 1882-5, and schedule of despatches sent 1882-4.
Rhodes House Library, Oxford (MSS Afr. s.5). Purchased from Francis Edwards Ltd 1931.

[44] **BULWER-LYTTON** (formerly **BULWER**), **Sir Edward George Earle Lytton** (1803-1873), 1st Bt 1838, 1st Baron Lytton 1866
Secretary of state for the colonies 1858-9.

Letters to him from colonial governors, statesmen and others 1858-9 (4 boxes); copies of letters from him 1859 (1 vol); corresp, notes, printed cabinet and parliamentary papers, etc rel to colonial affairs incl British N America 1839-60 (2 vols, 3 bundles, 4 items), the Ionian Islands 1850-61 (2 bundles), Australia and New Zealand 1853-64 (2 bundles), Africa 1854-9 (1 bundle) and misc 1838, 1857-70 (2 bundles, 12 items).
Hertfordshire RO (D/EK O1-16, 24-8). Deposited by his great-granddaughter Lady Cobbold 1953, 1962. NRA 4598.

See also *Cabinet Ministers*.

[45] **BUSBY, James** (1801-1871)
Resident in the North Island of New Zealand 1832-40.

Corresp, mainly official, 1830-70 (57 items); letters to his father and brothers 1823-39 (126 items); draft of the treaty of Waitangi, and related papers 1840 (1 bundle); MSS of his published works 1830-66 (7 bundles); speeches, press cuttings and misc papers (4 bundles).
Auckland Institute and Museum Library (MS 46). Presented by Mrs Wynne-Lewis 1956, 1958. NRA 25530.

Copies of his despatches to New South Wales 1833-9 (1 vol); MS 'Occupation of New Zealand 1833-43' (4 vols); MS 'History of New Zealand' (1 vol); diary and accounts 1868 (1 vol).
Alexander Turnbull Library, Wellington (MS sequence). Presented by William Busby 1929, except for diary presented by Mrs DF Hingston 1957.

Letters to him 1832-9 (2 vols).
National Archives of New Zealand, Wellington (BR 1-2).

Corresp and papers rel to his land claims in N Auckland 1853-74 (1 vol).
Auckland Public Library (NZ MSS 46). Presented by EN Ormiston 1936.

MS, proofs etc, of his pamphlet *The colonial question,* 1866 (10 items).
Alexander Turnbull Library, Wellington (Acc 75-317). Deposited by William Busby's daughter Mrs EA Williams 1975.

[46] **BUXTON, Sydney Charles** (1853-1934), Viscount Buxton 1914, Earl Buxton 1920
Parliamentary under secretary for the colonies 1892-5; governor-general of South Africa 1914-20.

Extensive general corresp, incl letters from Sir GS Barnes, Sir Henry Campbell-Bannerman, Viscount Grey, RB Haldane, Sir CEH Hobhouse, Lord Ripon, other politicians and friends *c*1888-1924; corresp and papers arranged by subject, incl Colonial Office, Post Office and Board of Trade *c*1876-1914 (50 bundles); corresp in S Africa with colonial secretaries, members of the royal household, S African officials, politicians and others, papers and press cuttings 1914-20, with misc letters rel to Colonial Office business etc 1892-1913 (25 bundles); press cuttings, printed works by him, and reviews 1878-1908 (several vols).
Mrs Elizabeth Clay (his granddaughter). *Guide to the papers of British cabinet ministers 1900-1951,* ed C Hazlehurst and C Woodland, 1974, pp26-7.

Testimonials presented to him as MP for Poplar 1912 (1 vol).
Tower Hamlets Central Library, Local History Library (No 60). Presented 1957.

[47] **BUXTON, Sir Thomas Fowell** (1837-1915), 3rd Bt 1858
Governor of South Australia 1895-8.

Diaries 1865-1915 (51 vols); household and personal accounts and bank books 1858-1909 (39 vols); addresses presented to him 1858, 1876, 1898 (3 items); photographs, press cuttings, etc, S Australia 1895-6 (1 vol).
Essex RO (D/DBx). Presented by JTA Burton Esq 1975. NRA 6835.

Misc addresses presented to him, photograph album and press cuttings book, S Australia 1895-8; scrap books rel to his public career in Britain.
Ronald de Bunsen Esq (his great-grandson).

CALEDON, Earl of, see Alexander.

CAMDEN, Marquess, see Pratt.

[48] CAMPBELL, Major-General Sir Archibald (1739-1791)
Lieutenant-governor of Jamaica 1779-82, governor 1782-5.

Corresp and papers rel to his military career in Canada, India and the American colonies 1760-79 (6 vols); copies of letters to Lord George Germain and others 1779-85 (1 vol); corresp with the War Office 1783-4 (1 vol); corresp with his Scottish trustees and others 1771-7 (5 vols); private letter book 1777-82 (1 vol); copies of letters to London 1780 (1 vol); Jamaica militia returns 1778-80 (1 vol); speech on opening the Jamaica assembly 1781 (2 copies); 'Memoir relative to the Island of Jamaica' 1782 (1 vol); general orders issued 1781-4 (2 vols); description by R Hodgson of the Spanish colonies in S America and W Indies nd (1 vol); misc corresp as governor of Madras 1785-8 (4 vols); journal of his financial transactions 1774-90 (1 vol); political accounts with John Moir 1776-89 (2 vols).
In family possession. Enquiries to NRA (Scotland). NRA 10123. Contemporary copies of his 'Memoir Relative to the Island of Jamaica' are in the British Library (King's MS 214), the National Army Museum (6807-180) and the Institute of Jamaica, Kingston (MS 16).

Corresp, letter books, minutes, orders, etc, Madras mainly 1785-9 (27 vols).
Scottish Record Office (GD 1/6). Deposited by Lieutenant-Colonel Duncan Campbell 1953. NRA 10123.

[49] CAMPBELL, Lieutenant-General Sir Archibald (1769-1843), 1st Bt 1831
Lieutenant-governor of New Brunswick 1831-7.

Copies of corresp with Lords Aberdeen and Glenelg and others mainly rel to disputes over crown lands 1832-6 (33 items).
Public Archives of Canada, Ottawa (MG24 A21). Acquired among the Delancey-Robinson collection 1918. NRA 25949.

Despatches from Glenelg 1835-8 (25 items).
New Brunswick Museum, Saint John (New Brunswick Historical Society Collection, shelf 27, packet 1).

[50] CAMPBELL, Lieutenant-General Sir James (1763-1819), Bt 1818
Civil commissioner for the Ionian Islands 1813-16.

Diary and corresp, Naples 1806 (1 vol); misc draft letters, Ionian Islands 1813-15.
In family possession. Enquiries to NRA (Scotland). NRA 10123.

[51] CAMPBELL, John Douglas Sutherland (1845-1914), styled Marquess of Lorne 1845-1900, 8th Duke of Argyll 1900
Governor-general of Canada 1878-83.

Letters from the Duke of Cambridge 1878-84 (16 items), Lord Kimberley 1880-3 (31 items) and Sir JA Macdonald 1879-90 (63 items); letters from British, Canadian and American statesmen, soldiers and others mainly rel to Canadian affairs and relations with the United States 1878-1902 (*c*4 bundles); family corresp 1876-83 (2 bundles).
The Duke of Argyll. Not open for research. A microfilm is in the Public Archives of Canada (MG27 IB4).

Letters from Sir JA Macdonald 1878-84 (1 vol); private secretary's letter book rel to his tour to the Canadian north west 1881; addresses presented to him 1881.
Public Archives of Canada, Ottawa (MG27 IB4).

CARADOC, see Cradock.

[52] CARDWELL, Edward (1813-1886), Viscount Cardwell 1874
Secretary of state for the colonies 1864-6.

Corresp with Lord Carnarvon, EJ Eyre, AC Hamilton-Gordon, Sir HK Storks and others 1864-7 (5 bundles); extracts from Colonial Office confidential print, proceedings of the royal commission on Jamaica, draft reports and other papers 1864-6 (2 bundles).
Public Record Office (PRO 30/48). Presented 1947 by his great-niece Mrs WE Rycroft, with additions by her brother Captain GD Fanshawe. NRA 20657.

See also *Cabinet Ministers*.

[53] CARINGTON (afterwards **WYNN-CARRINGTON**), **Charles Robert** (1843-1928), 3rd Baron Carrington 1868, Earl Carrington 1895, Marquess of Lincolnshire 1912
Governor of New South Wales 1885-90.

Letters from Australian and New Zealand governors, New South Wales statesmen and others mainly 1885-90; speeches, addresses, press cuttings and printed papers rel to Australian federation, defence, free trade, etc *c*1885-*c*1901; corresp with members of the royal family, incl telegrams from Queen Victoria while lord chamberlain 1892-5; general corresp 19th-20th cent, some rel to Australia; copies of political corresp 1876-1912, incl letters from Lord Knutsford and Edward Stanhope (2 vols); copies of his letters to his wife 1879-1918 (2 vols) and of other family corresp; speeches 1879-1918 (4 vols); diaries 1877-1928; his reminiscences

of and copies of his corresp with Edward VII 1855-
1910 (3 vols) and Lord Rosebery 1878-1912
(2 vols); recollections *c*1855-*c*1912 (2 vols); notes
and reminiscences rel to his governorship 1885-90
(several bundles); engagement diaries, visitors'
books, hunting diaries, scrapbooks and photograph
albums 19th-20th cent.
Brigadier AWA Llewellen Palmer (his grandson).
NRA 27389 (list of Australian papers); *Guide to the
papers of British cabinet ministers 1900-1951*, ed
C Hazlehurst and C Woodland, 1974, pp28-9.
Microfilms of all the papers are in the Bodleian
Library, Oxford (MSS Film 1097-1153), and of
those rel to Australia in the National Library of
Australia, Canberra (M917-32). Permission to use
the microfilms must be obtained from Brigadier
Llewellen Palmer.

[54] **CARLETON, General Guy** (1724-1808),
1st Baron Dorchester 1786
Lieutenant-governor of Quebec 1766-75, governor
1775-8: governor-in-chief of British North America
1786-96.

Many of his personal papers were destroyed by his
widow (Public Archives of Canada, *General
inventory: manuscripts*, iv, p59).

Papers of his headquarters as c-in-c America
1782-3, with earlier headquarters records 1775-82,
incl corresp with British ministers, military
commanders, colonial governors, American loyalists
and others, memoranda, warrants, returns,
accounts, etc (107 vols).
Public Record Office (PRO 30/55). Presented to the
Royal Institution in 1804 by John Symmons (who
had received them from Carleton's secretary
Maurice Morgann), purchased in 1930 by
JD Rockefeller Jr for the Colonial Williamsburg
Foundation, and presented by the Foundation to
HM The Queen 1957. NRA 23643; *HMC Report
on American Manuscripts in the Royal Institution of
Great Britain*, 4 vols, 1904-9.

Copies of letters from British ministers 1777-8
(1 vol); registers of his official letters 1776-8
(2 vols).
British Library (Add MSS 21698-700). Presented by
William Haldimand among the papers of Sir
Frederick Haldimand 1857.

Copies of letters from Lord Dartmouth and Lord
George Germain 1774-7 (1 vol).
Library of Congress, Washington (Force MSS).
Purchased 1867.

Letters from Brook Watson 1787 (12 items); copy
of his will 1808; misc letters, etc rel to him.
In private possession. NRA 1176.

[55] **CARLETON, General Thomas** (1735-1817)
Governor of New Brunswick 1784-6, lieutenant-
governor 1786-1817 (non-resident 1804-17).

Instructions 1784; letters 1785, nd (3 items);
military order book 1792-1813.

New Brunswick Museum, Saint John (Governor
Carleton CB Docs).

Copies of letters mainly to Robert Prescott 1796-9
(1 vol).
Montreal Historical Society. Transcripts are in the
Public Archives of Canada (MG23 D3).

Petition from electors of Saint John 1784, returns
of settlers in the Maritime Provinces 1784,
statement of his services 1810.
Public Archives of Canada, Ottawa (MG23 D3).

CARLINGFORD, Baron, see Fortescue.

[56] **CARMICHAEL, Major-General Hugh
Lyle** (1764-1813)
Governor of Tobago 1802; lieutenant-governor of
Demerara and Essequibo 1812-13.

Letter books, Jamaica and elsewhere in the
W Indies 1807-9, 1811 (3 vols).
Institute of Jamaica, Kingston (MS 14). Purchased
from Edward Hall, dealer, 1957-8. KE Ingram,
Sources of Jamaican history 1655-1838, i, 1976,
pp413-14.

[57] **CARMICHAEL SMYTH, Major-General
Sir James** (1779-1838), 1st Bt 1821
Governor of the Bahamas 1829-33; lieutenant-
governor of British Guiana 1833-6, governor
1836-8.

Entry book of misc letters, memoranda, reports, etc
1805-15; copies of despatches and letters sent as
colonial secretary, Cape Colony 1806-7 (3 vols);
journal 1806-7 (1 vol); reports, memoranda and
other papers rel to fortifications and ordnance in
the Netherlands, France, W Indies, Cape Colony,
British N America and Ireland 1813-28 (10 vols);
copies of despatches and letters sent, Bahamas
1829-33 (2 vols); copies of despatches sent, British
Guiana 1833-7 (3 vols); printed ordinances, British
Guiana 1831-5 (2 vols).
Public Record Office (PRO 30/35). Presented by
ECM Carmichael 1930, 1936. NRA 8650.

Letters from him to his wife while serving at
Cambrai 1818 and in British N America 1825, and
to his son from the Bahamas 1831-3, letters to him
from Lords Howick and Ripon 1833, brief account
of his career 1793-1819, papers as trustee of the
estate of General Francis Dundas 1818-27, will and
codicils 1820-2, and family corresp and papers
1785-1952 (9 vols, 309 items).
*William R Perkins Library, Duke University,
Durham, N Carolina*. Presented 1970. NRA 27882.

CARNARVON, Earl of, see Herbert HHM.

CASTLEREAGH, Viscount, see Stewart R.

[58] **CATHCART, General Charles Murray**
(1783-1859), styled Lord Greenock 1814-43,
2nd Earl Cathcart 1843
Administrator of Canada 1845-6; governor-in-chief
of British North America 1846-7.

Corresp and papers, British N America 1845-7, incl
letters from WE Gladstone, Lord Fitzroy Somerset
and the Duke of Wellington rel to defence, and his
letters patent and instructions as governor-in-chief
(5 bundles); copies of letters from him 1845-6
(1 vol); military corresp and papers 1803-45, 1849-
54 (11 bundles); family corresp 1798-1859 (11
bundles); notes and tables rel to communications in
British N America *c*1845 (1 vol); diary 1847 (1 vol).
Major-General the Earl Cathcart. NRA 3946 (A106-
8, C77-92, D128-38).

[59] **CATHCART, Major-General Sir George**
(1794-1854)
Governor of Cape Colony 1852-4.

Corresp, notebooks, autobiography, etc mainly rel
to his military career, incl service in British
N America and W Indies, 1810-51 (10 vols, 15
bundles); despatches from and draft despatches to
the secretary of state for the colonies 1852-4
(8 bundles); corresp with Sir George Clerk,
CH Darling, Lord Hardinge and other
administrators, statesmen, etc 1852-4 (8 bundles);
orders and instructions 1852, papers rel to
administration, commissariat, patronage, etc 1847-
54 (3 bundles); letter books 1852-4 (3 vols); journal
1852-4 (1 vol); addresses, etc presented to him
1852-3 (1 bundle); Crimean war papers 1854
(1 bundle); letters to his wife and brother, and other
personal papers 1794-1854 (14 bundles); maps,
plans and sketches *c*1812-*c*1854 (*c*8 vols and
bundles).
Major-General the Earl Cathcart. NRA 3946 (box
21).

[60] **CAVENAGH, General Sir Orfeur**
(1820-1891)
Governor of the Straits Settlements 1861-7.

Diaries 1859-67 (4 vols).
Major Orfeur Cavenagh.

[61] **CAVENDISH-BENTINCK** (formerly
BENTINCK), **William Henry** (1738-1809), styled
Marquess of Titchfield 1738-62, 3rd Duke of
Portland 1762
Secretary of state for home affairs 1794-1801.

Corresp as home secretary incl letters 1794-5 from
Henry Dundas (15 items), Sir Gilbert Elliot
(3 items), John King (12 items) and William
Windham (11 items); private letter books 1794-1801
(5 vols); corresp, memoranda, petitions, etc rel to
St Domingue 1793-9 (68 items); misc papers rel to
British N America 1794-early 19th cent (18 items)
and Corsica 1794 (7 items); printed addresses to Sir
Ralph Payne nd (1 bundle).

Nottingham University Library (Pw F, Pw V107-11).
Deposited by the 7th Duke of Portland 1949, 1968.
NRA 7628.

See also *Cabinet Ministers.*

[62] **CHAMBERLAIN, Joseph** (1836-1914)
Secretary of state for the colonies 1895-1903.

Corresp with Lords Grey, Loch, Milner and
Rosmead, Sir WF Hely-Hutchinson and others,
memoranda, Colonial Office minutes, etc rel to
S Africa 1879-1905, mainly the Jameson raid 1896-
7 and the Boer war 1899-1902 (*c*1,380 items);
corresp and papers rel to Australia, New Zealand
and the Pacific 1895-1905 (141 items), W Africa
mainly 1895-9 (131 items), W Indies 1895-1903 (98
items), Canada and Newfoundland 1897-1905 (over
250 items), and other colonies mainly 1895-1903
(*c*240 items); cabinet papers, confidential print, etc
mainly rel to S Africa 1896-1903 (784 items);
illuminated addresses, sketches, photographs, etc
during his and his wife's tour of S Africa 1902-3
(*c*42 vols and items); engagement book as secretary
of state 1903; press cuttings rel to colonial policy
1895-7 and the Jameson raid 1896-7.
Birmingham University Library (JC). Presented by
the Chamberlain family 1960. NRA 12604.

See also *Cabinet Ministers.*

CHELMSFORD, Baron, see Thesiger.

[63] **CHICHESTER, Lieutenant-Colonel Sir
Charles** (1795-1847)
Acting governor of Trinidad 1841-2, 1842-3.

Family and personal corresp 1811-45 (*c*12 bundles);
corresp registers 1842-5 (2 vols); letter books 1845-7
(2 vols); diaries 1822-5, 1835-47 (15 vols); hunting
diaries and lists of horses 1813-46 (4 vols);
commissions, addresses and other papers, mainly
Spain, W Indies and Canada, 1812-45 (6 bundles,
*c*17 items).
Brynmor Jones Library, Hull University (DDCH).
Deposited in the E Riding RO by his great-
granddaughter Mrs WL Bonaparte Wyse 1959, and
transferred 1974. NRA 6800.

[64] **CHILD-VILLIERS, Victor Albert George**
(1845-1915), 7th Earl of Jersey 1859
Governor of New South Wales 1890-3.

Corresp with British and Australian statesmen and
others 1888-94 (12 files).
National Library of Australia, Canberra (MS 2896).
Presented by the 9th Earl of Jersey 1971.

[65] **CHIPMAN, Ward** (1754-1824)
Administrator of New Brunswick 1823-4.

Corresp and papers of Chipman and his son Ward,
comprising general corresp and letter books 1767-
1842 (6 vols); political and official corresp and

papers 1777-1838, incl a few items as administrator
(3 vols); corresp, journals, reports, memoranda, etc
rel to New Brunswick boundary commissions
mainly 1796-8, 1816-30 (30 vols); corresp and
papers rel to legal business 1751-1844 (9 vols), land
settlement 1765-1842 (3 vols), missionary activities
1771-1835 (2 vols) and military affairs 1777-1804
(7 vols).
Public Archives of Canada, Ottawa (MG23 D1).
Purchased 1913. *General inventory: manuscripts*, iv,
pp39-42.

Personal, political and legal corresp, and papers rel
to the boundary question, land settlement, military
affairs, his assumption of the administration, etc
1783-1839 (c1,083 items).
New Brunswick Museum, Saint John (HT Hazen
Collection: Chipman Papers).

[66] CLARKE, Field Marshal Sir Alured
(1745-1832)
Lieutenant-governor of Jamaica 1782-90, of Lower
Canada 1791-3.

Letter book, Jamaica 1784-90; letter book and order
book, India 1799-1801; diaries 1825-9, 1831
(6 vols); misc papers (1 vol).
National Library of Wales (Rhual MSS 7, 10, 18-
23, 157, 160). Deposited by Mrs GH Heaton 1949.

Commissions and misc letters 1759-1802, 1830-1
(30 items).
Clwyd RO, Hawarden (Rhual MSS). Deposited by
Major BHP Heaton 1972. NRA 13672.

[67] CLARKSON, John (1764-1828)
Governor of Sierra Leone 1792.

Corresp and papers 1785-1828, mainly rel to
transport of freed slaves from Nova Scotia,
foundation of Sierra Leone, and his dispute with
the Sierra Leone Co 1791-8 (4 vols).
British Library (Add MSS 41262-4). Purchased
1925.

Journal Aug 1791-Mar 1792 (1 vol).
Howard University Library, Washington.

Journal Mar-Aug 1792 (1 vol); letters from settlers
1792-3 (18 items); corresp with King Naimbanna
1792 (6 items).
University of Illinois Library, Chicago (Sierra Leone
Collection). Acquired 1969-70. NRA 22949.

Journal Aug-Nov 1792 (1 vol).
Untraced. Printed in *Sierra Leone Studies*, viii, 1927.

Draft journal Aug-Nov 1791; letter book 1792.
Sierra Leone Public Archives, Freetown.

[68] CLIFFORD, Sir Hugh Charles (1866-1941)
Acting resident in Pahang 1890-1, 1893-6, resident
1896-9, 1901; governor of Labuan and North
Borneo 1899-1901, of the Gold Coast 1912-19, of
Nigeria 1919-25, of Ceylon 1925-7, of the Straits
Settlements 1927-9.

Corresp with secretaries of state, politicians,
colonial administrators, publishers, writers and
others 1887-1927 (6 vols); press cuttings rel to his
career and writings 1899-1927 (16 vols); memoir of
his family and early life (38pp).
H Clifford Holmes Esq.

[69] CLINTON, General Sir Henry (1730-1795)
Governor of Gibraltar 1794-5.

Papers of his headquarters as c-in-c America 1778-
82, with earlier headquarters records 1775-8, incl
official and semi-official corresp, letter books,
memoranda, warrants, returns, accounts, maps and
intercepted despatches, with his personal and family
corresp and papers 1750-1812, incl material rel to
his defence of his actions during the American war,
and the manuscript narrative of his campaigns
1775-82 (260 vols).
*William L Clements Library, University of Michigan,
Ann Arbor.* Purchased by Clements from Frances
Clinton 1925. *Guide to the English manuscripts*,
1942, pp46-65; RG Adams, *The headquarters papers
of the British army in North America during the
American revolution*, Ann Arbor 1926.

Letters to him and his sons mainly from admirals
1762-1828 (32 items).
Untraced. Sold at Christie's 19 Sept 1984, lot 230.

See also Carleton G.

[70] COCHRANE, Admiral Sir Alexander
Forrester Inglis (1758-1832)
Governor of Guadeloupe 1810-14.

Corresp and papers rel to the Egyptian campaign
1801 and his command of a squadron off Ferrol
1804-5 (5 vols); corresp, letter books, reports,
addresses, etc as c-in-c Leeward Islands station
1805-14, incl the capture and administration of
Guadeloupe and other French and Danish colonies
(15 vols); corresp, letter books etc as c-in-c
N American station 1813-15 (24 vols, 3 items);
naval corresp, mainly official, 1779-1824 (9 vols);
order books, signal books and other naval papers
1779-1815 (12 vols, 1 item); personal and family
corresp of him and his son Sir TJ Cochrane 1779-
1856 (32 vols).
National Library of Scotland (MSS 2264-97, 2309-
49, 2435-8, 2443-4, 2446-7, 2449-51, 2457, 2504,
2568-76, 2608, 3022; Ch 945-6). Presented by his
great-grandson the 2nd Baron Lamington 1935,
1938 and by the 3rd Baron Lamington 1942.
Catalogue of MSS, ii, pp67-76, 89-90, 160, 325.

[71] COCHRANE, Admiral of the Fleet Sir
Thomas John (1789-1872)
Governor of Newfoundland 1824-34.

Corresp rel to Newfoundland 1824-40 (1 vol); letter
books 1824-35 (14 vols); statistics, reports and other
papers, Newfoundland 1804-39 (5 vols); guest lists
1826-34 (8 vols); corresp, letter books, journals, etc,
E Indies station 1842-7 (72 vols, 1 item); corresp

and guest lists mainly as c-in-c Portsmouth 1852-5 (7 vols); signal books, logs and other naval papers 1798-1853 (19 vols); personal and family corresp of him and his father 1779-1856 (32 vols); registers of corresp 1812-52 (5 vols); private journals 1807-49 (28 vols); personal, household and estate corresp and papers 1809-54 (25 vols).
National Library of Scotland (MSS 2264-95, 2298-2308, 2350-2434, 2439-42, 2445, 2448, 2454-6, 2458-2503, 2505, 2577-2607). Presented by his grandson the 2nd Baron Lamington 1935, 1938. *Catalogue of MSS*, ii, pp67-78, 89-90.

[72] **COCKBURN, Admiral of the Fleet Sir George** (1772-1853), 8th Bt 1852
Governor of St Helena 1815-16.

Letter books 1794-1816, 1829-36, 1844-6, incl copies of letters from him to the Admiralty and to him from members of Napoleon Bonaparte's staff, St Helena 1815-16 (19 vols); log books 1788-1815 (18 vols); fleet orders 1794-1837 (12 vols); journals 1833-6 (3 vols); misc papers 1811-47 (5 vols).
Library of Congress, Washington. Purchased from dealers 1909, 1912. NRA 28001.

Diary 1797-1818, and papers rel to Bonaparte's imprisonment on St Helena (4 files).
National Maritime Museum (COC/1-12). Presented by Travers Buxton 1941.

[73] **CODRINGTON, General Sir William John** (1804-1884)
Governor of Gibraltar 1859-65.

Copies of corresp, orders and memoranda, mainly Gibraltar, 1859-68 (12 vols); copies of military corresp and reports on manoeuvres 1869-71 (1 vol); printed papers, Gibraltar 1864 (1 bundle).
Public Record Office (PRO 30/31). Presented by Sir AE Codrington 1922. NRA 8651.

Corresp, letter books and papers mainly rel to the Crimean war 1854-6, incl corresp with Lord Panmure and the commander-in-chief's office, diary of the embarkation from Balaklava 1856, memoranda and printed parliamentary papers (7 vols, 2 boxes).
National Army Museum (6807/375-81, 7808-90). Presented by the Royal United Service Institution 1968, and deposited by Major MCA Codrington 1978. NRA 20819.

[74] **COLBORNE, Field-Marshal John** (1778-1863), 1st Baron Seaton 1839
Lieutenant-governor of Upper Canada 1828-36; governor-in-chief of British North America 1838-9; high commissioner for the Ionian Islands 1843-9.

Despatches to and from secretaries of state for the colonies, corresp with provincial governors, army officers and others, reports, petitions, printed papers, etc, British N America mainly 1828-40, incl many items rel to the Canadian rebellions 1837-8 (*c*148 vols, bundles and items); corresp with Sir

Edmund Lyons, Sir HG Ward and others, despatches, memoranda etc, Ionian Islands mainly 1842-50 (*c*52 vols, bundles and items); military and misc corresp and papers 1806-63, incl his memoranda rel to the battle of Waterloo, and papers as lieutenant-governor of Guernsey 1825-8 and commander of the forces in Ireland 1855-60 (*c*80 vols, bundles and items); private corresp 1809-10, 1820-63, incl letters of introduction and congratulation, patronage applications, family corresp, etc (120 bundles); drafts and copies of letters sent 1829-30, 1837-62 (3 vols, 20 bundles).
Mrs Katherine Colborne Mackrell (widow of his great-grandson). NRA 5288. A microfilm of the papers rel to British N America is in the Public Archives of Canada, Ottawa (MG24 A40) and in the Seeley Memorial Library, Cambridge.

Letters mainly from General Sir GT Napier and General Sir WFP Napier 1819-54 (53 items).
William R Perkins Library, Duke University, Durham, N Carolina. Purchased 1965, 1975. NRA 27883.

[75] **COLE, General Sir Galbraith Lowry** (1772-1842)
Governor of Mauritius 1823-8, of Cape Colony 1828-33.

Military corresp and papers, Sicily, the Peninsula and France 1787-1817 (30 pieces); letter books 1823-8, corresp and misc papers, Mauritius 1822-9 (12 pieces); letter book 1828-32, corresp and misc papers, Cape Colony 1826-33 (5 pieces); personal and misc corresp and papers 1804-42 (11 pieces).
Public Record Office (PRO 30/43/48-105). Presented 1936-8 by Miss Mabel Lowry Cole. NRA 8661.

Misc military papers, Sicily, the Peninsula and France 1806-18 (38 items).
National Army Museum (6807/397). Presented by the Royal United Service Institution 1968. NRA 8661.

[76] **COLEBROOKE, General Sir William Macbean George** (1787-1870)
Lieutenant-governor of the Bahamas 1834-7; governor of the Leeward Islands 1837-41; lieutenant-governor of New Brunswick 1841-8; governor of British Guiana 1848 (did not proceed), of Barbados and the Windward Islands 1848-56.

Corresp and papers 1841-8, mainly rel to the Maine-New Brunswick boundary dispute (55 items).
Public Archives of Canada, Ottawa (MG24 A31). Acquired among the Delancey-Robinson collection 1918. NRA 25950.

Misc letters and petitions to him 1843-7 (14 items).
New Brunswick Museum, Saint John (Shelf 36, envelope 3).

Corresp, accounts, etc rel to family and financial affairs 1831-6 (3 bundles).
Kent AO (U791/E175,184,187). Deposited by the 4th Earl Sondes 1960. NRA 9144.

COLLEY, see Pomeroy-Colley.

[77] **COLLINS, Colonel David** (1756-1810)
Lieutenant-governor of Van Diemen's Land
1803-10.

Letters mainly from him to his family 1775-1810
(1 vol); misc papers, mainly New South Wales and
Van Diemen's Land, 1785-1810 (1 vol); family
corresp and papers 1746-1835 (2 vols).
Mitchell Library, Sydney (ML MSS 700). Acquired
1963 from his descendant John Trelawny-Ross.

[78] **COLUMBINE, Captain Edward Henry**
(d 1811)
Governor of Sierra Leone 1809-11.

Copies of corresp rel to survey of W African coast
1808-10 (1 vol); copies of corresp with the Colonial
Office, reports on tribes and slave trade, and notes
on social and economic affairs in Sierra Leone
1809-11 (3 vols); memoranda of his experiences as
governor 1809-11 (1 vol); journals 1809-10, 1811 (1
vol and 12pp); copies of journals of British envoys
to the interior 1802-6 (189pp).
University of Illinois Library, Chicago (Sierra Leone
Collection). Acquired 1969-70. NRA 22949.

Accounts as governor 1810-11 (1 roll).
Gloucestershire RO (D745/X5). Deposited by Judge
Woodcock 1951. NRA 14364.

[79] **COLVILE, Eden** (1819-1893)
Associate governor of Rupert's Land 1849-52.

Letters from Hudson's Bay Co officials 1850-2 (1
vol).
Provincial Archives of Manitoba, Winnipeg (HBCA
D7). Deposited among the Hudson's Bay Co
archives 1971.

[80] **COLVILLE, General Sir Charles**
(1770-1843)
Governor of Mauritius 1828-32.

Corresp 1784-1843, incl letters from his father, and
from the Duke of Wellington and others; letter and
order books, corresp and papers rel to his military
service in Egypt, the Peninsula and France 1800-
18; letters to him as c-in-c Bombay from
Mountstuart Elphinstone and Lord Hastings 1819-
27; instructions, indentures and other papers,
Mauritius 1828; travel accounts, Egypt 1820 and
Bombay to the Red Sea 1821.
The Viscount Colville of Culross. Enquiries to NRA
(Scotland). NRA 10112.

COMBERMERE, Viscount, see Cotton.

[81] **COOTE, General Sir Eyre** (1762-1823)
Governor of Jamaica 1805-8.

Corresp and papers, Jamaica 1805-8, comprising
corresp (9 bundles), letter books (4 vols), notebooks

(5 vols), military orders, copies of addresses and
replies, reports rel to Jamaica and the Spanish
American colonies, etc (5 vols, 7 bundles); corresp,
letter books, orders, etc, Ireland and N America
1775-82 (19 vols and bundles), England and Ireland
1783-93 (14 vols and bundles), W Indies 1793-4 (5
vols, 2 items), Ireland, Netherlands, Egypt and
England 1794-1805 (*c*50 vols, *c*40 bundles and
items), Walcheren and the Peninsula 1809-14 (15
vols, 14 bundles); misc papers incl commissions,
diaries 1784, 1790-1800, and a statement of services
1774-1809 (12 vols, *c*20 bundles and items).
Untraced. Sold by his descendant JAC Sykes at
Sotheby's 13 Mar 1979, lot 99. NRA 20791.

[82] **CORYNDON, Sir Robert Thorne**
(1870-1925)
Resident in Barotseland 1897-1900; administrator of
North Western Rhodesia 1900-7; resident
commissioner for Swaziland 1907-16, for
Basutoland 1916-17; governor of Uganda 1917-22;
governor of Kenya and high commissioner for
Zanzibar 1922-5.

Corresp, memoranda, reports and printed papers rel
to agriculture, Indian settlers, native reserves,
transport and communications, etc, Uganda and
Kenya, mainly 1918-24 (39 files); personal corresp
1897-1925 (1 file); personal financial papers 1907-24
(5 files); notes and reminiscences, copies of articles,
and other biographical and literary papers 1887-
1928 (7 files).
Rhodes House Library, Oxford (MSS Afr. s.633).
Presented through CG Richards 1966. NRA 13760.

[83] **COTTON** (afterwards **STAPLETON-
COTTON**), **Field-Marshal Sir Stapleton**
(1773-1865), 6th Bt 1809, 1st Baron Combermere
1814, 1st Viscount Combermere 1827
Governor of Barbados 1816-20.

The correspondence printed in *Memoirs and
correspondence of Field Marshal Viscount
Combermere, GCB, etc, from his family papers, by
the Right Hon Mary, Viscountess Combermere, and
Capt WW Knollys*, 2 vols 1865, has not been
traced.

Letters from the Duke of Wellington 1810-23 (2
vols); corresp rel to the siege of Bhurtpore 1825-6
(1 vol); original papers, transcripts and text 1808-30
omitted from *Memoirs and correspondence*, incl misc
letters, speeches, addresses, etc, Barbados 1817-20
(5 files).
National Army Museum (7203-25, 8408-114).
Deposited by the 5th Viscount Combermere 1972,
1984.

Corresp, memoranda, etc mainly as c-in-c India
1825-30 (36 items).
Chester City RO (CR 72/29/135-70). Deposited by
the Chester Archaeological Society. NRA 16683.

[84] **COURTNEY, Leonard Henry** (1832-1918),
Baron Courtney of Penwith 1906
Parliamentary under secretary for the colonies
1881-2.

Political and general corresp 1862-1918, incl a few
letters to him as colonial under secretary (10 vols);
corresp with family and friends 1857-83 (2 vols);
letter books 1885-1910 (2 vols); misc papers incl
printed speeches, pamphlets etc, and list of leading
articles for *The Times* 1864-c1918 (4 vols).
*British Library of Political and Economic Science,
London* (R(SR)1003). Presented by Beatrice Webb
1937.

Letters to him and his family rel to politics and
administration in Great Britain, Canada and New
Zealand 1863-1919 (109 items).
*William R Perkins Library, Duke University,
Durham, N Carolina.*

[85] **COWPER, Sir Charles** (1807-1875)
Administrator of New South Wales 1857, 1859.

Corresp and papers 1856-72, mainly letters from
governors, political colleagues and others, with
some draft replies and memoranda (3 vols);
commissions, addresses and misc papers 1856-70 (1
vol); misc letters and papers 1847-57 (1 bundle).
Mitchell Library, Sydney (Ac 16, A 676-8, *D 60).

[86] **CRADOCK** (afterwards **CARADOC**),
General John Francis (1759-1839), 1st Baron
Howden 1819
Lieutenant-governor of Gibraltar 1809-10; governor
of Cape Colony 1811-14.

Copies of corresp rel to the sepoy mutiny, Madras
1806 (1 vol), and with Sir John Moore and others,
Portugal and Gibraltar 1808-9 (3 vols); corresp with
Lord Castlereagh and others 1809 (1 vol); copies of
letters mainly to Lords Liverpool and Bathurst and
to colonial officials, Cape Colony 1811-14 (6 vols);
reports, minutes and proclamations, Cape Colony
1806-14 (4 vols); sketch book, India nd.
Captain JW Alston-Roberts-West. NRA 4349.

[87] **CRAIG, General Sir James Henry**
(1748-1812)
Governor of Cape Colony 1795-7; governor-in-chief
of British North America 1807-12.

Letters received as adjutant-general in the
Netherlands 1794-5.
British Library (Add MSS 46702 ff6-198 *passim*,
46703 f258, 46706 ff1-231 *passim*, 46707 f15,
46711 ff189, 191). Presented among the papers of
Sir George Don by Miss AC De Lautour 1948.

Copies of his letters to Henry Dundas and
memoranda rel to defence of Cape Colony, etc
1795-7 (1 vol).
Public Record Office of Northern Ireland (D2431/5/
14). Deposited among the papers of the 2nd Earl of
Caledon by the Trustees of the Caledon Estates
1969. NRA 13276.

Copies of his corresp, Cape Colony 1795-7 (1 vol).
University of Witwatersrand, Johannesburg (A24).

Copies of letters to the secretary of state for the
colonies while commanding the army in the
Mediterranean 1805-6 (1 vol).
British Library (Add MS 20176). Purchased among
the papers of Sir Hudson Lowe 1854.

[88] **CRAUFURD, Colonel James** (d 1811)
Governor of Bermuda 1794-6.

Copies of letters to the Duke of Portland, Lord
Spencer and others 1795-6 (2 vols); misc corresp
1796-7 (9 items); declaration of support from
inhabitants of Bermuda 1797.
Bermuda Archives, Hamilton. Purchased at
Sotheby's 29 June 1982, lot 164.

CRAWFORD, Earl of, see Lindsay.

[89] **CRAWFURD, John** (1783-1868)
Resident in Singapore 1823-6.

Misc papers rel to commerce, history and customs
of Java, Singapore, Penang, etc c1811-21; draft
report of his embassy to Siam and Cochin China
1822 (1 vol).
British Library (Add MS 33411). Purchased 1888.

Draft 'Description of India' incl accounts of the
arts, economy, etc [1832-3] (1 vol).
India Office Library and Records (MSS Eur D
457/B).

Dictionary of English and Javanese (2 vols).
British Library (Add MSS 18577-8). Purchased
1851.

[90] **CUNYNGHAME, General Sir Arthur
Augustus Thurlow** (1812-1884)
Lieutenant-governor of Cape Colony 1877-8.

Corresp with JH Brand, Sir HBE Frere, Lord
Hardinge, Sir GJ Wolseley and others, memoranda,
printed papers, etc 1854, 1873-84, mainly S Africa
1874-8 (c110 items).
In family possession. A microfilm is in the National
Army Museum (7805-42). NRA 18641.

Corresp with Major HG Elliott, Colonel J Eustace
and Sir HBE Frere, and misc papers, 1877-8 (1
bundle).
National Army Museum (6807-386-1). Presented
among the papers of his successor, Lord
Chelmsford.

DALHOUSIE, Earl of, see Ramsay.

[91] **DALLAS, Alexander Grant** (1816-1882)
Governor-in-chief of Rupert's Land 1862-4.

Letters from Edward Ellice 1859-63 (7 items);
travel journals 1837-40, 1853-5 (5 vols); notes and

press cuttings (44pp); sketches and photographs (2 vols).
Provincial Archives of British Columbia, Victoria (Add MSS 73, 745).

Corresp mainly rel to Hudson's Bay Co business 1858-64 (1 vol).
Provincial Archives of Manitoba, Winnipeg (HBCA D8). Deposited among the Hudson's Bay Co archives 1971.

[92] **DALRYMPLE, General Sir Hew Whitefoord** (1750-1830), 1st Bt 1815
Lieutenant-governor of Gibraltar 1806-8.

Letters mainly from Major William Cox on attachment to the Spanish junta 1808 (1 vol).
British Library (Add MS 50827). Purchased 1961.

Papers rel to military business and the peace of Cintra 1808-10 (1 bundle).
Major-General the Earl Cathcart. NRA 3946 (C98).

Letters from Lord Collingwood 1806-7 (22 items).
Untraced. Sold at Sotheby's 15 Oct 1956, lot 1956.

[93] **DARLEY, Sir Frederick Matthew** (1830-1910)
Lieutenant-governor of New South Wales 1891-1910.

Family and personal letters to him, letters from him to his wife, and other corresp 1860-1905 (3 bundles).
In private possession. Photocopies are in the National Library of Australia, Canberra (MS 5545).

Misc corresp and papers, mainly personal and business letters to him 1875-1905 (1 bundle).
Mitchell Library, Sydney (ML MSS 2157/1).

[94] **DARLING, General Sir Ralph** (1775-1858)
Acting governor of Mauritius 1819-20, 1823; governor of New South Wales 1825-31.

Commissions, incl one for his father, 1786-1848 (18 items).
National Library of Australia, Canberra (MS 3439). Bequeathed by Sir JA Ferguson 1971.

Letters from his wife and Sir Henry Hardinge, with other family corresp of Lady Darling, 1832-6, 1850 (1 vol).
Mitchell Library, Sydney (ML MSS 2566). Purchased 1973.

[95] **DAVEY, Lieutenant-Colonel Thomas** (1758-1823)
Lieutenant-governor of Van Diemen's Land 1812-17.

Register of government and general orders issued by him 1813-16 (1 vol).
British Library (Add MS 37840). Purchased 1909.

[96] **DENISON, Lieutenant-General Sir William Thomas** (1804-1871)
Lieutenant-governor of Van Diemen's Land 1846-55; governor of New South Wales and governor-general of the Australian colonies 1854-61.

Letters from the Duke of Newcastle, Sir Charles Wood and others 1852-66 (11 items); copies of letters from him mainly rel to official business 1846-64, with a few letters to him (6 vols); letters from him to his sons 1855-63 (44 items), and copies of his letters to them 1855-6 (1 vol); journal of his visit to Norfolk Island 1857 (1 vol); appointments 1819, 1860, 1868.
Mrs Pamela Goedhuis (widow of Colonel WME Denison) NRA 24584 (partial list). Microfilms of sections of the papers are in the India Office Library and Records (reel 670), the National Library of Australia (M606-7), Nottingham University Library (De Wm) and Rhodes House Library, Oxford (Micr. Austr. 1).

Corresp mainly with Henry Labouchere 1856-7 (1 bundle).
National Library of Australia, Canberra (MS 1957).

DERBY, Earls of, see Stanley.

[97] **DESBARRES, Joseph Frederic Wallet** (1722-1824)
Lieutenant-governor of Cape Breton 1784-7, of Prince Edward Island 1805-12.

Corresp and papers rel to his estates and his career as surveyor and administrator, with later family papers, 1762-1894 (28 vols); corresp, memoranda, accounts, etc of him and his secretary Thomas Ashfield 1784-1829 (2 vols); reports on his estates 1795 (1 vol).
Public Archives of Canada, Ottawa (MG23 F1). Acquired 1922-58.

[98] **DE WINTON, Major-General Sir Francis Walter** (1835-1901)
Commissioner for Swaziland 1889, for British East Africa 1890-1.

Letter book as private secretary to Lord Lorne, rel to Lorne's tour to the Canadian north west 1881.
Public Archives of Canada, Ottawa (MG27 IB4, vol 2).

Corresp with Leopold II, King of the Belgians, and misc papers 1884-9 (24 items).
Musée Royal de l'Afrique Centrale, Brussels (RG 840). Marcel Luwel, *Sir Francis De Winton, administrateur général du Congo 1884-86*, Brussels 1964.

[99] **DONKIN, General Sir Rufane Shawe** (1773-1841)
Acting governor of Cape Colony 1820-1.

Copies of semi-official and private letters as acting
governor and c-in-c, Cape Colony 1820-1 (1 vol).
Port Elizabeth City Library, Cape Province.
Purchased from a London dealer 1927.

DORCHESTER, Baron, see Carleton G.

[100] **DOUGLAS, General Sir Howard**
(1776-1861), 3rd Bt 1809
Lieutenant-governor of New Brunswick 1823-31;
high commissioner for the Ionian Islands 1835-40.

Copies of letters from him, Royal Military College
1812-18 (1 vol), New Brunswick 1823-30 (2 vols),
Ionian Islands 1835-41 (1 vol).
*Harriet Irving Library, University of New
Brunswick, Fredericton* (BC-MS). Presented by the
1st Baron Beaverbrook.

Letters, despatches and papers 1816-59 (1 vol);
letter books 1824-30 (2 vols).
Public Archives of Canada, Ottawa (MG24 A3).
Acquired 1927, 1931.

Letters and papers rel to Sir James Carmichael
Smyth's report on New Brunswick's defences 1827
(54pp).
Metropolitan Toronto Library.

Journal 1795 (1 vol).
In private possession. A photocopy is in the Public
Archives of Canada (MG24 A3, vol 5).

[101] **DOUGLAS, Sir James** (1803-1877)
Governor of Vancouver Island 1851-64, of British
Columbia 1858-64.

Corresp and letter books rel to the fur trade,
administration of Vancouver Island and British
Columbia, his claims against the United States
government, etc 1840-74; messages on opening and
proroguing the Vancouver Island assembly 1858-64;
commissions, instructions and other formal papers
nd; accounts, invoices and notes 1825-72; notebooks
and press cuttings 1830-c1875; diaries and travel
journals 1827-77.
Provincial Archives of British Columbia, Victoria.

[102] **DOUGLAS, William Bloomfield**
(1822-1906)
Administrator of the Northern Territory of
Australia 1870-3; resident in Selangor 1876-82.

Diaries, S Africa to Australia 1854, Northern
Territory 1872, Selangor 1876-82.
E Douglas Potter Esq. JM Gullick, 'The Bloomfield
Douglas diary', *Journal of the Malayan Branch of
the Royal Asiatic Society*, xlviii, pt 2, 1975, pp1-51.

[103] **DOYLE, General Sir Charles Hastings**
(1805-1883)
Lieutenant-governor of New Brunswick 1866-7, of
Nova Scotia 1867-73.

Corresp and papers 1833-83, incl misc letters,
addresses and press cuttings, New Brunswick and
Nova Scotia 1861-73, papers rel to his military
career 1833-61, and letters from the royal family
1871-83 (1 vol, c90 items).
Bodleian Library, Oxford (MSS North). Presented
by the Pilgrim Trust 1932, following purchase
from his great-nephew the 12th Baron North. NRA
0837.

[104] **DRUMMOND, General Sir Gordon**
(1772-1854)
Administrator of Upper Canada 1813-15, of Lower
Canada 1815-16.

Copies of his letters to Captain Noah Freer and Sir
George Prevost 1813-14 (1 vol).
Public Archives of Canada, Ottawa (MG24 A41).
Acquired 1965.

[105] **DUCKWORTH, Admiral Sir John
Thomas** (1748-1817), 1st Bt 1813
Governor of Newfoundland 1810-12.

His papers were sold at Sotheby's 15 Feb 1937, lots
1-216 (property of Sir GHJ Duckworth-King Bt),
27 Oct 1947, lots 145-64, 14 Nov 1955, lots 1059-
61 and 24 July 1978, lot 111. They were widely
dispersed, and the present location of some has not
been traced.

Official and private corresp, reports, orders,
addresses, etc 1790-1813; letter books 1800-7, 1812
(6 vols); log book 1779-80; order and standing order
books 1800-6 (6 vols); journals 1805, 1807-8, 1810-
12 (3 vols).
National Maritime Museum (DUC). Mainly
purchased at Sotheby's 1937-9, 1966.

Military and civil corresp, letter books, journals,
fishery and shipping statistics, etc, Newfoundland
1810-12, with a few earlier and later papers.
*Provincial Archives of Newfoundland and Labrador,
St John's* (P1/5). Purchased c1970.

Letters from William Baker, George Morey and
others, memoranda, accounts etc c1785-1817 (c320
items); copies of letters received and sent 1793-1812
(10 vols).
*Beinecke Library, Yale University, New Haven,
Connecticut* (Osborn Collection). Purchased from
dealers 1940-72. NRA 18661.

Letters from the Admiralty, military and naval
officers, merchants and others, memoranda, reports
on captures of American vessels, etc, Newfoundland
1810-12 (c110 items).
Public Archives of Canada, Ottawa (MG24 A45).
Acquired c1976. NRA 25952.

Corresp with his captains, reports, standing orders,
etc, Newfoundland 1810-12 (c70 items).
*Department of Special Collections, University of
Chicago Library, Illinois.* Presented by FW Jay
1927, and purchased subsequently. *National union
catalog*, MS 64-80.

Letters to his wife and rel to naval business 1788-1816, returns of vessels under his command 1809 (23pp).
Queen's University Archives, Kingston, Ontario. Purchased 1971.

Letters and papers, Minorca 1798-9, and congratulatory letter from council of St Kitts on his victory off St Domingue 1806 (10 items).
Hispanic Society of America, New York (HC 363/19).

Letters from Lord Nelson 1799 (14 items).
National Maritime Museum (Sutcliffe-Smith Collection). Purchased from AE Sutcliffe-Smith 1976.

Letters to him, invoices, accounts, contracts, etc 1801-15, mainly while serving in the Caribbean 1801-6 (c100 items).
University of the West Indies Library, Kingston, Jamaica. KE Ingram, *Sources of Jamaican history 1655-1838*, i, 1976, p450.

Letters from Sir George Nugent, with a few copies of replies, 1801-5 (1 vol).
Rhodes House Library, Oxford (MSS W. Ind. s.11). Purchased from a dealer by whom they had been acquired at the 1937 sale.

Letters to and from him, commission as c-in-c Jamaica station, etc 1801-6 (23 items).
University of Florida Library, Gainesville.

Corresp mainly with Vice-Admiral Sir Charles Stirling 1803-10 (84 items).
Rice University Library, Houston, Texas. Purchased 1953-65. *National union catalog*, MS 80-2192.

Letters from the Duke of Northumberland 1807-9 (11 items).
The Duke of Northumberland. Purchased from Maggs Bros. NRA 0836 (1978 list, G/5).

DUFFERIN AND AVA, Marquess of, see Hamilton-Temple-Blackwood.

[106] **DUNDAS, Henry** (1742-1811), 1st Viscount Melville 1802
Secretary of state for home affairs 1791-4, for war 1794-1801.

Corresp and papers rel to slavery, estates, military operations etc in the W Indies, incl letters from Sir Ralph Abercromby, c1790-1811 (3 vols); rel to Canadian convoys, finances, trade, Newfoundland fisheries and penal colony, etc, incl letters from governors and officials 1787-c1811 (4 vols); rel to Penang, Malacca, Sumatra and other territories in SE Asia and the Pacific 1762-1811 (1 vol).
National Library of Scotland (MSS 1051, 1068, 1075, 3835, 3847-50). Purchased 1931-48.
Catalogue of manuscripts, i, pp142, 144-5 and ii, pp302-3, 306.

Corresp and papers rel to colonial affairs, mainly rel to defence and military operations, incl Cape Colony 1785-1810 (c20 items), Ceylon 1795-1809 (3 vols, etc), Malta 1798-1807 (c40 items) and the W Indies 1790-1808 (c40 items).
Scottish Record Office (GD 51). Deposited 1951, 1971 by Mrs GB Sanderson, formerly the Hon Mrs Robert Dundas, on behalf of the 9th Viscount Melville, with some papers added by Mr and Mrs Macbeth of Dunira. NRA 10188.

Corresp and papers mainly rel to Indian and E India Co affairs, incl calendars of letters from St Helena and Cape Colony, and of papers rel to the War and Colonial Office and to the colonial agent for Ceylon 18th-19th cent (2 vols).
John Rylands University Library of Manchester (Eng MSS 697-8). Acquired c1930-9.

Letters mainly to the 1st and 2nd Viscounts Melville rel to the W Indies 1781-1830 (2 vols).
Rhodes House Library, Oxford (MSS W. Ind. s.7, 8).

Misc corresp 1782-1810 (3 vols, c50 items).
Houghton Library, Harvard University, Cambridge, Massachusetts (MS Eng 777, 777.1, 777.2, bMS Eng 1327, fMS Can 18). Deposited by Harvard University Committee on Research in the Social Sciences c1930, with additional material presented by LM Friedman 1945 (Sotheby's 26 Apr 1926, lot 141), and purchased from a dealer 1952. NRA 24376.

Corresp and papers rel to S Africa c1791-1801.
Cape Archives Depot, Cape Town (Acc 455).

See also *Cabinet Ministers.*

DUNMORE, Earl of, see Murray J.

[107] **DUNN, Thomas** (1729-1818)
Administrator of Lower Canada 1805-7, 1811.

Letter book 1805-7.
Château de Ramezay, Montreal.

[108] **D'URBAN, Lieutenant-General Sir Benjamin** (1777-1849)
Governor of Antigua 1820-5; lieutenant-governor of Demerara and Essequibo 1824-31; governor of British Guiana 1831-3, of Cape Colony 1833-8.

Corresp, journals, reports, orders, maps, etc rel to the Peninsular war and his service in the Portuguese army 1808-16 (1,307 vols, bundles and items).
National Army Museum (7805-46). Deposited 1978 by a descendant, JL Sunnucks. NRA 23422.

Letters to him 1823-47 (9 vols); copies of despatches to secretaries of state for the colonies 1834-8 (5 vols); corresp rel to the Cape frontier 1835 and copies of despatches to the lieutenant-governor of the eastern Cape 1836-7 (3 vols); civil, military and misc letter books 1834-8 (7 vols); copies of letters sent 1828-46 (2 vols); memoranda books 1834-46 (2 vols); general orders 1834-8 (6 vols); military returns and misc papers 1832-40 (1 vol); newspapers and press cuttings 1835-47 (3 vols).

Cape Archives Depot, Cape Town (A 519). Presented by WSM D'Urban 1911. NRA 28119.

Letters and papers to and from him, incl some typescript copies, 1835-49 (42 items).
Cory Library for Historical Research, Rhodes University, Grahamstown, Cape Province (MSS 6768-6809). Presented by the estate of BA Steer.

DURHAM, Earl of, see Lambton.

ELGIN, Earl of, see Bruce.

[109] ELIOTT, General George Augustus (1717-1790), 1st Baron Heathfield 1787
Governor of Gibraltar 1776-90.

Corresp and papers mainly Gibraltar 1759, 1776-89 (46 items); letter book *c*1743; official letter book 1785-7; official diary 1782-5 (1 vol); general orders, Ireland 1774-5 and Gibraltar 1782-7 (2 vols); account in Spanish of the siege of Gibraltar 1782 (1 vol); brief account of the siege by his steward 1783; commission as major-general 1759; quitroll as governor 1789-90.
Devon RO (346M/F102-48,160-1, O10,15-19). Deposited 1957 by RA Meyrick among the Drake family papers (Eliott was brother-in-law to Sir FH Drake Bt). NRA 6713.

Corresp and orders mainly rel to the siege of Gibraltar 1779-83 (3 boxes).
National Maritime Museum (ELL). Presented by Sir James Caird, who had purchased them in 1941 from the 5th Earl of Minto, a distant relation of Eliott.

Day book kept during the siege of Gibraltar by his ADC Thomas Paterson, containing accounts of operations, extracts from orders, etc 1779-80.
British Library (Add MS 45188). Presented 1938 by WA Raper; formerly owned by Eliott's son-in-law JT Fuller.

[110] ELLIOT, Admiral Sir Charles (1801-1875)
Governor of Bermuda 1846-54, of Trinidad 1854-6, of St Helena 1863-70.

Official corresp 1856-70, general corresp 1856-74, letters to his son Frederick 1867-74, Elliot and Ouseley family and legal papers 1851-1901, addresses, official printed papers, etc (2 boxes); notes on Demerara 1831, papers rel to W Indian slavery 1832-3, memoranda and other papers rel to China 1840-2, etc (1 box); misc diplomatic corresp 1841-6, and family corresp 1763-1892 (2 boxes).
National Library of Scotland (Accs 5534, 7287). Purchased 1972, and at Sotheby's 16 Oct 1978, lot 209. NRA 18510.

[111] ELLIOT (afterwards **ELLIOT-MURRAY-KYNYNMOUND**), **Sir Gilbert** (1751-1814), 4th Bt 1777, 1st Baron Minto 1797, 1st Earl of Minto 1813

Viceroy of Corsica 1794-6.

Official corresp, Toulon and Corsica 1793-6, corresp with Lord Nelson and Lady Hamilton, account of the seizure and defence of Toulon 1793, journal 1794, and misc papers (62 vols, etc).
National Maritime Museum (ELL/100-66). Presented by Sir James Caird, who had purchased them from the 5th Earl of Minto in 1941.

Corresp with the British government 1794-6 (1 vol), with Pasquale Paoli 1793-5 (1 vol); letters from CA Pozzo di Borgo 1794-1822 (172ff); corresp with and rel to émigrés from France and Corsica 1794-1806 (2 vols); general corresp, mainly Corsica 1793-7 (2 vols); corresp with his wife 1793-9 (5 vols); financial and misc papers, Toulon and Corsica 1793-8 (2 vols).
National Library of Scotland (MSS 11049-50, 11071-3, 11209-16, 11224 ff1-172). Purchased from the 5th Earl of Minto 1958, 1960. NRA 10476.

See also *Diplomats*.

[112] ELLIOT, Hugh (1752-1830)
Governor of Barbados 1807-8, of the Leeward Islands 1808-14.

Letters to him from secretaries of state for the colonies 1809-13, from him to his secretary Philip Heydinger 1811-13, and general corresp, Leeward Islands 1813 (1 vol); drafts and copies of despatches from him 1809-13 (3 vols); papers rel to legal cases against planters for cruelty to slaves, addresses and petitions, etc 1810-13 (1 vol); general corresp 1807-14 (1 vol); corresp with his wife 1793, 1802-13, and journal 1810-11 (1 vol).
National Library of Scotland (MSS 12960, 13005, 13054-8). Purchased from the 5th Earl of Minto 1958, 1960. NRA 10476.

See also *Diplomats*.

[113] ELLIOT, Admiral John (1732-1808)
Governor of Newfoundland 1786-9.

Corresp with his nephew the 1st Earl of Minto 1781-1805 and with Sir David and Lady Carnegie 1799-1808 (1 vol); general corresp 1770-1806, some rel to Newfoundland (1 vol); naval notes 1780, *c*1786-9 (1 vol); notes of corresp during election campaign 1796 (1 vol); financial, legal and estate corresp and papers 1724-1815 (17 vols); naval commissions 1758-1805 (6 items).
National Library of Scotland (MSS 12865-84, 13355, Ch 10421-6). Purchased from the 5th Earl of Minto 1958, 1960. NRA 10476.

Letters to him from Lords Barham and Sandwich and others, and letters from him to his father and brother Gilbert 1745-1805 (1 vol).
National Maritime Museum (ELL). Presented by Sir James Caird, who had purchased them from the 5th Earl of Minto in 1941.

Letter book and memorandum and order book kept while commanding in the Mediterranean 1780 (2 vols).

The Earl of Southesk. Enquiries to NRA (Scotland). NRA 10554.

Orders and instructions to Prince William Henry on appointment as deputy governor of Newfoundland and as captain of HMS *Pegasus* 1786 (c118pp).
Newfoundland Provincial Reference Library, St John's.

[114] **ELLIOT, Sir Thomas Frederick** (1808-1880)
Assistant under secretary for the colonies 1847-68.

Corresp with Sir Henry Taylor and others mainly rel to Colonial Office business 1828-78 (3 vols); travel journals, Europe 1826-7 and Ireland and Scotland 1837 (3 vols); engagement diaries 1840, 1844, 1849, 1865, 1868-9 (6 vols); misc papers 1828-30 (1 vol); commonplace book nd.
National Library of Scotland (MSS 19420-33). Presented by HWA Elliot 1967 and by his widow 1977.

[115] **ELLIOT-MURRAY-KYNYNMOUND, Gilbert John** (1845-1914), styled Viscount Melgund 1859-91, 4th Earl of Minto 1891
Governor-general of Canada 1898-1904.

Corresp and papers as military secretary to Lord Lansdowne in Canada 1883-6, incl employment of Canadian troops for imperial service, and the Riel rebellion (7 vols); corresp as governor-general with the royal family, British and Canadian statesmen, soldiers and others incl Sir FW Borden, Sir ETH Hutton, Sir Wilfrid Laurier and Sir RW Scott, memoranda of conversations with Laurier and others, and misc papers, Canada 1896-1913, mainly 1898-1904 (22 vols); letter books 1898-1904 (5 vols); press cuttings 1898-1905 (5 vols); corresp and papers as viceroy of India 1905-10 and rel to India 1899-1913 (216 vols); corresp, notebooks and papers rel to his military career and interests 1867-1913 (34 vols); corresp rel to Roxburghshire politics and local affairs 1869-1913 (4 vols); general and misc corresp 1854-1914 (34 vols); family corresp 1847-1913 (13 vols); diaries, travel journals and notebooks 1858-1913 (52 vols); misc political papers 1873, 1886, 1892 (1 vol); legal and financial papers 1876-1913 (6 vols); military commissions 1870-92 (8 items); addresses presented to him and his wife 1898-1904, 1909-10, nd (139 items).
National Library of Scotland (MSS 12365-12411, 12473-12803, 13354, 13378-94, 13412-14, Ch 10413-20, 10495-10633). Purchased from the 5th Earl of Minto 1958, 1966. NRA 10476.

Letters from his brother Arthur c1852, 1884-1913 (5 vols).
National Library of Scotland (MSS 19473-7). Presented by his nephew HWA Elliot 1967.

[116] **EYRE, Edward John** (1815-1901)
Lieutenant-governor of New Munster 1846-53, of St Vincent 1854-60; acting governor of Jamaica 1861-4, governor 1864-6.

Corresp with Edward Cardwell, Sir HS Giffard, members of the Eyre family and others 1835-1901 (56 items); memorandum of his services, addresses to him, legal documents and printed papers rel to his defence of his conduct in Jamaica, 1860-8 (1 vol, 17 items); testimonials in his favour 1856-7 and misc personal papers 1840-51 (16 items).
State Library of South Australia Archives Department, Adelaide (PRG 177). Purchased from KA Webster 1966. NRA 27636.

MS autobiography 1832-9, written 1859, with two letters to him from Thomas Carlyle 1866, 1869 (1 vol).
Mitchell Library, Sydney (A 1806). Purchased from Henry Stevens, Son & Stiles 1932.

Entry book of minutes of letters from him to Alfred Domett 1848-50.
National Archives of New Zealand, Wellington (NM 6/1). Presented by his grandson Lieutenant-Colonel ARG Gordon 1949.

[117] **EYRE, Major-General Sir William** (1805-1859)
Administrator of Canada 1857.

Corresp and papers rel to his military career 1839-53 (2 boxes), and to the Crimean war 1854-6 (4 boxes); corresp and papers, British N America 1841-59, mainly as c-in-c 1856-9, incl corresp with the governor-in-chief, the War Office, etc, addresses to him, returns of the forces in the N American colonies, papers rel to defence of the Red River settlement, and misc letters and papers as civil administrator 1857 (11 boxes); letter book and order book 1856-9 (2 vols); journals 1854-6 (4 vols); printed papers 1837-58 (1 box).
Public Record Office (PRO 30/46). Partly presented to the War Office by Dr CRB Eyre 1938, and partly to the PRO by Mrs Mary Eyre 1939. NRA 23457.

[118] **FANNING, General Edmund** (1737-1818)
Lieutenant-governor of Nova Scotia 1783-6, of Prince Edward Island 1786-1804.

Petitions, depositions, affidavits and replies to charges against him and two of his officials 1789-92, incl two letters from him to Evan Nepean 1791 (2 vols).
Public Archives of Canada, Ottawa (MG23 E5). Acquired 1921, 1923.

Papers rel to the Prince Edward Island Fencibles 1796-1808 (11 items).
William R Perkins Library, Duke University, Durham, N Carolina. Acquired 1957.

[119] **FARQUHAR, Sir Robert Townsend** (1776-1830), 1st Bt 1821
Governor of Penang 1804-5, of Réunion 1810-11, of Mauritius 1810-11, 1811-17, 1820-3.

Memorial and papers rel to his governorship of Penang 1798-1806 (20 items).
Huntington Library, San Marino, California.

[120] **FERGUSSON, Sir James** (1832-1907), 6th Bt 1849
Governor of South Australia 1869-73, of New Zealand 1873-5.

Memorandum book 1869-72 (1 vol); copies of minutes 1869-70 (1 vol).
State Library of South Australia Archives Department, Adelaide (GRG 2/18/6-7). Deposited among the Governor's Office records 1978.

See also *Diplomats.*

[121] **FINLAYSON, Duncan** (1796?-1862)
Governor of Assiniboia 1839-44.

Journals as a chief factor in the Hudson's Bay Co 1831-8 (3 vols).
Provincial Archives of Manitoba, Winnipeg (HBCA E12). Deposited among the Hudson's Bay Co archives 1971.

[122] **FINNISS, Boyle Travers** (1807-1893)
Administrator of South Australia 1854-5, of the Northern Territory 1864-6.

Journals of his voyages from Britain to S Australia 1836 and from the Northern Territory to S Australia 1866 (2 vols); journal of the Northern Territory survey expedition 1865 (1 vol); notebooks 1856-7, 1876 and nd (42 vols); corresp, letter book, etc rel to Port Darwin cable station 1871-2; misc corresp and papers 1835-91.
State Library of South Australia Archives Department, Adelaide.

[123] **FITZGERALD, Captain Charles** (1791-1887)
Governor of the Gambia 1844-7, of Western Australia 1847-55.

Copies of his despatches 1844-51 (2 vols, 1 item); copies of statistical returns to the Colonial Office, Gambia 1846 (1 vol).
Northamptonshire RO (E(GB)943-6). Deposited 1931 with the Northamptonshire Record Society by his great-nephew Colonel RGGJ Elwes. NRA 23057.

Copies of his despatches 1852-4 (1 vol).
Mitchell Library, Sydney (A 832). Purchased 1920 from Dymock, bookseller, Sydney.

[124] **FITZROY, Sir Charles Augustus** (1796-1858)
Lieutenant-governor of Prince Edward Island 1837-41; governor of the Leeward Islands 1841-6, of New South Wales 1846-55; governor-general of the Australian colonies 1851-5.

Speeches to the New South Wales legislative council signed by him 1846-54 (164pp).
Mitchell Library, Sydney (A 706).

Visitors' book 1849-52.
Mitchell Library, Sydney (ML MS 2477).

Testimonials from the Synod of Australia, the University of Sydney, and inhabitants of New South Wales 1855 (55pp).
National Library of Australia, Canberra (MS 1106). Presented by Mrs EG St Aubyn c1963.

[125] **FORTESCUE** (afterwards **PARKINSON-FORTESCUE**), **Chichester Samuel** (1823-1898), Baron Carlingford 1874, 2nd Baron Clermont 1887
Parliamentary under secretary for the colonies 1857-8, 1859-65.

Political corresp with WE Gladstone, Lord Spencer and others 1854-90 (496 items); diaries 1851-65 (6 vols).
Somerset RO (DD/SH). Bequeathed in 1973 by his great-nephew the 2nd Baron Strachie. NRA 8898.

See also *Cabinet Ministers.*

[126] **FOVEAUX, Lieutenant-General Joseph** (1765-1846)
Acting lieutenant-governor of Norfolk Island 1800-1, lieutenant-governor 1801-4; administrator of New South Wales 1808-9.

Copies of his despatches to PG King 1800-4 (1 vol); remarks c1809 rel to the settlement of New South Wales and Van Diemen's Land, and misc papers 1796-1806 (1 bundle).
Mitchell Library, Sydney (A 1444, Af 48). Purchased from Angus & Robertson, booksellers, Sydney 1920.

Letter book 1808-9.
Archives Office of New South Wales, Sydney (7/2730). Transferred from the Mitchell Library 1967.

[127] **FOX, General the Hon Henry Edward** (1755-1811)
Governor of Minorca 1801-2; lieutenant-governor of Gibraltar 1804-6.

Letters to him and misc papers mainly rel to affairs in the Mediterranean 1802-7 (1 vol, etc).
British Library (Add MSS 37050, 37053). Purchased with papers of his son-in-law Sir HE Bunbury Bt 1905.

Letter book, N America 1783.
Harriet Irving Library, University of New Brunswick, Fredericton (MG H2). Deposited among the papers of Edward Winslow.

Letter book, Minorca 1802 (1 vol).
Wigan RO (D/DZ EHC13). Presented by Edward Hall 1949.

See also *Diplomats.*

[128] **FRANKLIN, Rear-Admiral Sir John**
(1786-1847)
Lieutenant-governor of Van Diemen's Land 1836-
43.

Corresp with his family, naval officers, explorers
and others 1801-45, incl a few items rel to Van
Diemen's Land 1838-44 (*c*270 items); letter books
1819-21, 1823-7, 1831-3 (5 vols); journals 1818,
1820-1, 1823-8, 1830-2, 1835, 1841 (14 vols, 30pp);
log, HMS *Bellerophon* 1807 (1 vol); statements of
naval services 1807-22 (1 vol); astronomical
observations 1819 (1 vol); memoranda on
administration of Van Diemen's Land 1839-43 (9
items); misc letters, notes and papers mainly rel to
Arctic exploration 1818-40 (200pp).
Scott Polar Research Institute, Cambridge (MS 248).
Bequeathed by Miss Jessie Lefroy 1941.
Manuscripts in the Scott Polar Research Institute,
pp274-92.

Corresp with John Richardson and others 1812-45
(over 200 items); journal 1821-2 (1 vol).
Mrs PVW Gell (widow of his great-grandson). NRA
5438.

Letters from Sir Thomas Briggs 1831-40 (1 vol),
from GW Crowe and JC Robinson 1832-7 (1 vol).
British Library (Add MSS 46868, 47768). Presented
by the Scott Polar Research Institute 1949, 1952.

Letters to him, introducing settlers and visitors to
Van Diemen's Land 1836-8 (1 vol).
Mitchell Library, Sydney (A 1570). Acquired 1922.

Magnetic observations in N America 1825-6 (1 vol).
British Library (Add MS 22613). Acquired 1856.

Letters from him to his wife 1839-41 (9 items);
addresses to him 1837, 1843 (3 items); papers rel to
the Tasmanian Society 1841 (5 items); misc papers
of his wife, incl a dinner engagement book 1837-43
and rough travel journals *c*1838, 1843-4.
University of Tasmania Library, Hobart (Royal
Society of Tasmania MSS 16-18). Mainly presented
by WF Rawnsley 1923 and by the Scott Polar
Research Institute 1948. Access by application to
the Secretary, Royal Society of Tasmania, GPO
Box 1166, Hobart, Tasmania 7001.

[129] **FRERE, Sir Henry Bartle Edward**
(1815-1884), 1st Bt 1876
Governor of Cape Colony and high commissioner
for South Africa 1877-80.

Copies of corresp of him and his wife mainly with
HEG Bulwer, Sir ME Hicks Beach and Queen
Victoria 1862, 1878-80, 1884 (72 items); addresses,
petitions and resolutions presented to him 1877-83,
with some copies of replies (2 vols, 166 items);
'Treasure and curiosity book', 'Household book'
and 'In memoriam' 1871 (3 vols).
South African Library, Cape Town (MSB 197).
Presented by the South African Museum 1950.
NRA 28121.

Addresses and misc papers, S Africa 1879-81 (6
bundles and items).

India Office Library and Records (MSS Eur F
81/41-5). Presented by P Frere 1944-5. NRA 27516.

Notes on African affairs and constitutions.
London University Library (MSS 947-9).

Private corresp 1869-80 (1 bundle).
Public Record Office (CO 959/1).

See also *Diplomats*.

[130] **FYANS, Foster** (1790-1870)
Administrator of Norfolk Island 1834.

Reminiscences 1810-*c*1843, written *c*1854 (1 vol).
La Trobe Library, Melbourne (VSL MS 6939).
Presented by Mrs KG Neill 1962.

Letters to him 1832-47, diary 1858-60, etc (1
bundle).
Mitchell Library, Sydney (Uncat MS Set 507).
Acquired 1938.

Narrative of his experiences in Victoria 1837-53,
with other notes and drafts (1 vol).
Mitchell Library, Sydney (A 2059). Acquired from
DC Walker 1939.

Letters to him, accounts and legal papers 1844-
*c*1864 (*c*100 items).
In private possession. Photocopies are in the La
Trobe Library (MS 10594).

[131] **GAWLER, Colonel George** (1796-1869)
Governor of South Australia 1838-41.

Instructions 1838 (28pp); appointment as
commissioner of public lands 1838; letter from
Lord John Russell and other corresp 1838-49 (6
items); memorials and addresses to him 1838, 1841
(12 items); misc papers 1839-41 (8 items);
commissions and military papers 1810-49 (12
items); school exercise book 1804.
*State Library of South Australia Archives
Department, Adelaide* (PRG 50). Presented by his
great-granddaughter Mrs PB Warcup 1952 and by
Dr DR Gawler 1955. NRA 27635.

[132] **GIPPS, Sir George** (1791-1847)
Governor of New South Wales 1837-46.

Letters from CJ La Trobe, mainly rel to land sales
in the Melbourne area, 1840-5 (1 vol).
Dixson Library, Sydney (MS 259). Bequeathed by
Sir William Dixson 1952.

Speeches to the New South Wales legislative
council signed by him 1842-6 (60pp).
Mitchell Library, Sydney (A 706).

[133] **GLADSTONE, William Ewart** (1809-1898)
Parliamentary under secretary for war and the
colonies 1835, secretary of state 1845-6; high
commissioner for the Ionian Islands 1858-9.

Special corresp 1828-98, incl corresp with Lord
Lisgar 1846-72 (188ff), Lord Lytton 1858-65

(1 vol), Lord Stanmore 1851-96 (4 vols), and with Lords Derby, Granville, Kimberley and Ripon as secretaries of state for the colonies in his administrations 1868-94 (10 vols); general corresp 1834-5 (1 vol), as secretary of state 1845-6 (2 vols), and as high commissioner 1858-9, incl letters from Sir HK Storks (2 vols); copies of letters from him 1835-53 (2 vols), and rel to the Ionian Islands 1858-9 (2 vols); register of letters received while secretary of state 1845-6 (1 vol); memoranda rel to the defence of Canada, convicts in Australia, etc 1845-6 (1 vol), to the Ionian Islands, etc 1858-9 (2 vols) and to pensions for colonial governors, Canadian defence, Ionian Islands finances, etc 1864 (1 vol).
British Library (Add MSS 44141-2, 44166-7, 44179, 44224-7, 44237, 44241, 44287, 44319-22, 44354, 44363-4, 44390-1, 44527-8, 44550-1, 44556, 44735, 44747-8, 44753). Presented by the Gladstone Trustees 1935.

Addresses presented to him as high commissioner, with other papers rel to the Ionian Islands 1852-63 (*c*3 boxes).
St Deiniol's Library, Hawarden (Glynne-Gladstone MSS). Deposited by Sir EW Gladstone Bt 1968. Access through Clwyd RO. NRA 14174.

Corresp with Queen Victoria 1845-6 (1 bundle); draft reports to her rel to the Ionian Islands 1858-9 (99ff).
British Library (MS Loan 73/2-3). Deposited by AC Gladstone 1931. NRA 21658.

Journals 1834-5, 1844-6 incl brief notes of Colonial Office business, meetings with governors and reading on colonial subjects (2 vols); journal 1857-9, incl brief notes of corresp, discussions and visits as high commissioner (1 vol).
Lambeth Palace Library (MSS 1422, 1427, 1434). Deposited by his sons 1928. NRA 21424.

See also *Cabinet Ministers.*

GLASGOW, Earl of, see Boyle.

[134] GLOVER, Captain Sir John Hawley (1829-1885)
Lieutenant-governor of Lagos 1863, 1864-6, administrator 1866-70, 1871-2; governor of Newfoundland 1876-81, 1883-5, of the Leeward Islands 1881-3.

Corresp with the 5th Duke of Newcastle, Sir John Pope Hennessy, Lord Russell, Sir GJ Wolseley and others, memoranda, petitions, etc 1861-78 (10 files); letter books 1873-5 (2 vols); proceedings of Lagos vice-admiralty court nd (1 file); orders issued by him during the Volta expedition 1873-4 (1 vol); papers rel to the Ashanti war and Volta expedition 1873-4 (4 vols, 2 files).
Royal Commonwealth Society. Presented by his daughter Mrs R Fairfax 1927. NRA 6389; *Manuscript catalogue,* p85.

GODERICH, Viscount, see Robinson FJ.

[135] GORDON (formerly **HAMILTON-GORDON**), **John Campbell** (1847-1934), 7th Earl of Aberdeen 1870, 1st Marquess of Aberdeen and Temair 1916
Governor-general of Canada 1893-8.

General corresp and misc papers rel to education, patronage, social engagements, tours, etc, Canada 1893-8 (19 bundles); corresp and misc papers of him and his wife rel to British politics, Scottish local affairs, his lord lieutenancy of Ireland, social reform, family matters, etc *c*1863-*c*1934 (3 vols, *c*22 bundles); corresp and papers rel to his British Columbia estate 1890-5 (2 bundles), and letters from his estate manager in Scotland 1894-8 (6 bundles); accounts as lord lieutenant of Ireland 1906-14 (8 vols).
The Haddo Trustees. Enquiries to NRA (Scotland). NRA 9758. A microfilm of the Canadian correspondence is in the Public Archives of Canada (MG27 IB5).

Corresp of him and his wife 1890-1939, mainly during his term as governor-general and with Canadian friends after their return to Britain, incl many letters from Sir Wilfrid Laurier and WL Mackenzie King, and misc addresses and papers (6 vols); press cuttings 1893-9 (17 vols).
Public Archives of Canada, Ottawa (MG27 IB5, vols 1-5, 14-31). Presented by his daughter, the Dowager Lady Pentland 1951.

GORMANSTON, Viscount, see Preston.

GOSFORD, Earl of, see Acheson.

[136] GOULBURN, Henry (1784-1856)
Under secretary for the colonies 1812-16, for war and the colonies 1816-21.

Misc copies of despatches, etc 1814-26 (1 bundle); secret service accounts and related papers 1812-21 (1 bundle); letters to him from Robert Peel 1812-24 (1 bundle); letters from him to his mother 1809-14 (1 bundle); corresp with his wife 1813-16, 1821, 1839 (*c*500 items); memoirs 1807-*c*1827.
Surrey RO, Kingston-upon-Thames (Acc 319). Deposited by Major-General EH Goulburn 1951. NRA 0777.

See also *Cabinet Ministers.*

[137] GRAHAM, Colonel Robert (1816-1887)
Deputy governor of British Kaffraria 1864-8.

Letters from Sir PE Wodehouse 1864-8 (79 items); misc corresp and papers of members of the Graham family 1773-1900, incl letters from Sir George Cathcart 1852-4, Sir HGW Smith 1848-59, Sir PE Wodehouse 1865-8 and Major-General RH Wynyard 1861 (4 vols); papers rel to his career

in S Africa 1851-76 and misc private papers 1846-71 (52 items).
Major JJ Graham of Fintry. NRA 23600 (5-7, 10/90-2, 14/60).

[138] **GRANT, Sir John Peter** (1807-1893)
Governor of Jamaica 1866-73.

Corresp and papers as a civil servant in Bengal 1827-62, incl letters from Lord Dalhousie 1848-58 and Lord Canning 1856-62 (23 vols and bundles); corresp, petitions and misc papers, Jamaica 1866-74 (6 bundles and items); personal corresp 1826-68 (5 bundles); family corresp 1842-91 (9 bundles); business corresp and papers 1840-61 (1 vol, 2 bundles); misc papers 1869-93 (4 bundles); pamphlets and parliamentary papers 1857-91, some rel to Jamaica (12 items).
India Office Library and Records (MSS Eur F 127/1-62). Deposited by his grandson James Strachey 1965. NRA 27528.

General corresp of him and his wife, and of his daughter and son-in-law Sir JW Colvile, arranged alphabetically 1834-1916, incl letters to him from Lords Canning, Dalhousie and Macaulay (3 vols).
British Library (Add MSS 60632-4). Purchased among papers of the Strachey family 1978.

[139] **GRANT DUFF, Sir Mountstuart Elphinstone** (1829-1906)
Parliamentary under secretary for the colonies 1880-1.

Letters from statesmen, colonial governors, authors and others 1855-1905, incl Lords Brassey, Dufferin, Kimberley and Roberts (32 vols); unbound corresp, papers rel to his governorship of Madras 1881-6, and engagement diaries.
Mrs Sheila Sokolov Grant (his granddaughter). Enquiries to the Historical Manuscripts Commission. NRA 24627 (bound corresp only).

GRANVILLE, Earl, see Leveson-Gower.

[140] **GREGORY, Sir William Henry** (1817-1892)
Governor of Ceylon 1872-7.

Corresp, addresses, speeches and other papers rel to British politics, Ceylon, his artistic and literary interests etc c1835-1890, incl letters from Lord Carnarvon, Sir AC Hamilton-Gordon, Sir JD Hooker, Lord Kimberley, Sir AH Layard, Sir JR Longden, Sir Robert Peel, Sir HGR Robinson, Lord Russell, Sir WRW Wilde and others (several thousand items).
In family possession.

[141] **GRENFELL, Field-Marshal Francis Wallace** (1841-1925), 1st Baron Grenfell 1902
Governor of Malta 1899-1903.

Congratulatory letters to him following battle of Toski 1889; letters from Lord Kitchener c1896-9, from Lord Salisbury 1899-1903, and from various correspondents during S African war and first world war; diaries 1874-1925 (51 vols); drafts of his memoirs (20 vols); photograph albums and scrapbooks containing letters, press cuttings, etc, incl material rel to Egypt and Malta.
In private possession.

[142] **GRENVILLE, Richard Plantagenet Campbell Temple-Nugent-Brydges-Chandos-** (1823-1889), styled Earl Temple 1823-39 and Marquess of Chandos 1839-61, 3rd Duke of Buckingham and Chandos 1861
Secretary of state for the colonies 1867-8.

Corresp c1846-89, incl some rel to Colonial Office business 1867-8 and as governor of Madras 1875-80 (1,763 items); letter books 1855-7, 1867-8, 1878-80 (10 vols); corresp and papers rel to Buckinghamshire elections and local defence c1846-89 (several hundred items); letters, reports, press cuttings, etc, India 1858-85 (c580 items); diaries 1847-8, 1868, 1880-1 (3 vols); appointments diaries 1867-8 (2 vols); notebooks c1855, 1880-1 (5 vols).
Huntington Library, San Marino, California. Purchased 1925 after sale in 1921 by his daughter Baroness Kinloss. *Guide to British historical manuscripts in the Huntington Library*.

Corresp mainly with cabinet colleagues and with Lord Monck rel to Fenian activities in the United States and Canada 1867-8 (2 vols).
British Library (Add MSS 41860, 43742). Acquired by gift and purchase from the Revd GWT Tyndale-Biscoe 1929, 1934.

Letters from Lord Belmore rel to the attempted assassination of the Duke of Edinburgh 1868, and related papers (10 vols).
Dixson Library, Sydney (MS Q 23-32). Bequeathed by Sir William Dixson 1952.

Political and personal corresp and papers 1846-84, mainly 1866-7 (c120 items).
Buckinghamshire RO (AR 40/63(L)). Deposited by his grandson HN Morgan-Grenville 1963. NRA 25231.

Political and personal corresp and papers 1846-84, incl corresp with Queen Victoria 1866-75 (c100 items).
RRG Close Smith Esq (his great-great-grandson). NRA 25231. Photocopies are in Buckinghamshire RO.

[143] **GRENVILLE, William Wyndham** (1759-1834), Baron Grenville 1790
Secretary of state for home affairs 1789-91.

Royal corresp 1789-92 (2 vols); corresp with Henry Dundas 1784-91 (1 vol), William Pitt 1783-93 (1 vol), William Windham 1806-7 (2 vols), and Sir George Nugent, JG Simcoe and other colonial officials 1789-1829 (2 vols); corresp and papers rel to British N America 1760-1813 incl précis of minutes of legislatures 1788-90 and memoranda on trade and exploration (8 vols), to W Indies 1764-1817 (4 vols), to E Indies and Australia 1766-1813 (6 vols), and to the slave trade 1788-1817 (1 vol). *British Library* (Add MSS 58855-6, 58906, 58914, 58930-1, 59004-5, 59230-47, 59305). Purchased 1970 from the executors of GG Fortescue, a descendant of his nephew GM Fortescue.

Lists of colonial officials, their appointments and salaries *c*1790 (1 vol); election accounts 1784, 1790. *Huntington Library, San Marino, California.* Purchased 1925 after sale in 1921 by his great-great-great niece Baroness Kinloss.

See also *Cabinet Ministers.*

[144] GREY, Albert Henry George (1851-1917), 4th Earl Grey 1894
Administrator of Southern Rhodesia 1896-7; governor-general of Canada 1904-11.

Corresp and papers *c*1880-1917 rel to Rhodesia, S Africa, Canada, his business ventures, church reform, proportional representation, public house trusts, university extension, etc, incl letters from Joseph Chamberlain, Lords Elgin, Milner and Minto, and CJ Rhodes (135 boxes); notebooks and scrapbooks (27 boxes).
Durham University Department of Palaeography and Diplomatic (Grey of Howick Collection). Deposited by the 5th Earl Grey 1955.

Corresp with the royal family 1905-11 (2 vols), with secretaries of state for the colonies 1904-11 (6 vols), with Sir Wilfrid Laurier 1904-11 (5 vols), with James Bryce and others rel to Canadian-American relations 1906-11 (5 vols), rel to the formation of Alberta and Saskatchewan 1905 (1 vol), and rel to Newfoundland 1906-11 (2 vols); misc corresp 1904-6 (1 vol); printed papers 1905-11 (1 vol).
Public Archives of Canada, Ottawa (MG27 IIB2, vols 1-23). Presented by the 5th Earl Grey 1955.

Corresp and misc papers of him and his wife mainly rel to Southern Rhodesia 1893-9, incl letters from him to her 1896-7 (1,063ff).
National Archives of Zimbabwe, Harare (GR 1/1). *Guide to the historical manuscripts in the National Archives of Rhodesia*, pp174-82.

Letters to him from Major H Craufurd and others rel to the public house trust movement 1900-2, among the papers of the 2nd Earl of Lytton (1 file). *Lady Cobbold* (Lytton's daughter). NRA 25520.

[145] GREY, Sir Charles Edward (1785-1865)
Governor of Barbados and the Windward Islands 1841-6, of Jamaica 1846-53.

Corresp and misc papers 1825-64, incl letters from Lord William Bentinck 1825-9, Lord Glenelg 1835-50, Lord Gosford 1835-7, Sir George Grey 1835-7, Lord Grey 1846-52, 1864 and Lord John Russell 1839-41 (*c*480 items); reports and memoranda (mainly drafts and copies), India 1829-33, Canada 1836, Jamaica 1852 (*c*20 items); commissions and

instructions 1830-52 (8 items); journal, China and voyage home 1832 (1 vol); election address 1837; misc notes and other papers *c*1855-65 (4 bundles). *Bodleian Library, Oxford.* Presented 1986 by his great-granddaughter Mrs BD Rennison.

[146] GREY, Sir George (1812-1898)
Governor of South Australia 1840-5, of New Zealand 1845-54, 1861-7, of Cape Colony 1854-61.

Corresp with British and colonial statesmen and politicians, colonial governors, military and naval officers, churchmen, authors and others 1833-98 (*c*3,030 items); letter book 1845-53; visitors' books 1861-5 (2 vols).
Auckland Public Library (Grey Collection). Mainly presented by him from 1887. NRA 28105.

Letters from politicians, administrators and others rel to S Africa 1851-97 (*c*590 items); journals of expeditions in Australia 1837-9 (2 vols); sketches by him (1 box).
South African Library, Cape Town (MSB 223). Presented by Auckland Public Library 1955. NRA 28123.

Copies of despatches to Lord Grey mainly rel to land claims of members of the Church Missionary Society 1847-51 (1 vol).
Alexander Turnbull Library, Wellington (qMS sequence). Purchased from KA Webster 1966.

Journal kept during his walk from Gantheaume Bay to Perth 1839, vocabulary of dialects of SW Australia 1840, and misc corresp 1844-91 (1 file). *Mitchell Library, Sydney* (Ag 12). Purchased from various sources 1936-9.

[147] GREY, Henry George (1802-1894), styled Viscount Howick 1807-45, 3rd Earl Grey 1845
Parliamentary under secretary for war and the colonies 1830-3, secretary of state 1846-52.

Political and personal corresp 1818-94, incl many letters to and from Sir Henry Barkly, Sir James Brooke, Sir WMG Colebrooke, Sir WT Denison, Sir RW Gardiner, Sir CE Grey, Lord Harris, Sir JM Higginson, Sir HGW Smith, Sir HEF Young and other colonial governors mainly 1846-52 (*c*14,000 items), with letters, memoranda, reports, pamphlets and other enclosures *c*1830-94 (*c*6,180 items); private letter book as under secretary 1831-3; register of Colonial Office corresp 1846-52; memoranda, minutes, draft bills, etc rel to colonial affairs, mainly arranged by colony or subject, 1823-93 (1 vol, 10 files, 584 items); colonial patronage register 1846-51; journals 1827-30, 1833-71 (29 vols); printed papers, Lower Canada 1836-7 (3 vols).
Durham University Department of Palaeography and Diplomatic (Grey of Howick Collection). Deposited by the 5th Earl Grey 1955-63, and by the 6th Earl Grey 1967-73. NRA 6228.

Letters from Lord Elgin 1846-52 (6 vols); draft letters to Elgin 1846-52 (2 vols); corresp, memoranda and other papers rel to emigration

1823-50, British N America 1824, 1846-52, the navigation laws, his *Colonial policy of Lord John Russell's administration* (1853), etc (4 vols). *Public Archives of Canada, Ottawa* (MG24 A10, vols 21-32). Presented by the 4th Earl Grey while governor-general of Canada.

See also *Cabinet Ministers*.

[148] **GRIFFITH, Sir Samuel Walker** (1845-1920)
Lieutenant-governor of Queensland 1899-1903.

Corresp mainly with statesmen and governors of Queensland 1886-1920 (3 vols); memoranda, reports, addresses, etc rel to political, legal and social questions 1887-1919 (1 vol); personal papers 1851-1920, incl diaries and notebooks 1854-1919, family corresp 1873-1920, and genealogical corresp 1866-1919 (3 vols, 1 box); literary and business papers and legal judgements 1862-1920 (3 vols); commissions, printed papers, photographs, etc 1862-1922 (5 vols, 2 boxes).
Mitchell Library, Sydney (ML MSS 363). Presented by his daughters 1951.

Corresp rel to private affairs 1860-8 (1 vol), and to public affairs 1869-1904 (7 vols); diaries 1862-1915 (53 vols); misc papers *c*1860-1891 (3 vols).
Dixson Library, Sydney (MSQ 184-98, MS 145). Bequeathed by Sir William Dixson 1952. NRA 25545.

Lecture notes 1862 (2 vols).
National Library of Australia, Canberra (MS 3461). Bequeathed by Sir JA Ferguson 1971.

Papers rel to his translation of Dante's *Divina Commedia* (1912).
Mitchell Library, Sydney (Uncat MS Set 293).

[149] **GROSE, Lieutenant-General Francis** (*c*1758-1814)
Lieutenant-governor of New South Wales 1789-94.

Misc letters, commissions and papers 1775-1800 (1 bundle).
Mitchell Library, Sydney (Ag 31). Purchased in part from Angus & Robertson, booksellers, Sydney 1912.

[150] **GUDGEON, Colonel Walter Edward** (1842-1920)
Resident commissioner for the Cook Islands 1898-1901.

Autobiography, with related papers incl Maori genealogies, 1842-1910.
Dr Elsdon Craig. A microfilm is in the Alexander Turnbull Library, Wellington (Micro MS 811).

Misc papers 1898-*c*1909, incl letter to Lord Ranfurly and message to Cook Islands parliament 1898, Cook Islands genealogies, and articles on the London Missionary Society.
Hocken Library, University of Otago, Dunedin (MS v622/A-H).

Genealogies mainly of North Island Maoris, with index and vocabulary, compiled *c*1875-*c*1910 (1 vol). *Auckland Institute and Museum Library* (MS 128). Purchased 1948.

GUILFORD, Earls of, see North.

[151] **HALDIMAND, Lieutenant-General Sir Frederick** (1718-1791)
Governor of Quebec 1777-85.

Corresp with military commanders, colonial governors and others, reports, general orders, etc during his service in Canada, Florida and New York 1758-77 (40 vols); corresp with British ministers and government departments 1777-86, incl some copies of corresp of his predecessors 1760-78 (24 vols); corresp with c-in-c America 1777-83 (3 vols), with governors and military commanders in Nova Scotia 1777-84 (2 vols), with his lieutenant-governors 1778-84 (1 vol), with officers commanding forts in Quebec and on the Great Lakes 1778-85 (30 vols), and with officers of Royal Engineers, German Legion, loyalist regiments and militia, mainly 1776-84 (23 vols); corresp and papers rel to civil administration in Quebec 1768-88 (10 vols), to the Canadian provincial navy 1775-84 (6 vols), to Indian affairs 1777-84 (14 vols), to prisoners of war 1777-84 (14 vols), to the quartermaster-general's and commissary-general's departments 1778-84 (10 vols), and to the case of John Cochrane 1778-84 (5 vols); misc corresp with soldiers, officials and inhabitants of Quebec 1777-91 (13 vols); registers of letters from the Quebec adjutant-general's office 1778-83 (3 vols), of general orders issued 1776-84 (2 vols), of military warrants issued 1778-84 (9 vols), and of commissions granted 1778-84 (1 vol); minutes of the governor's council 1777-84 (2 vols); memorials addressed to him 1777-85 (7 vols); misc papers rel to Quebec 1771-87, incl inventories of his papers as governor (9 vols); private memoranda 1756-78 (1 vol); diaries 1786-90 (3 vols).
British Library (Add MSS 21661-892). Presented by William Haldimand 1857.

[152] **HAMILTON, Major-General Alexander Mark Kerr** (d 1842)
Superintendent of British Honduras 1806-9.

Letter and order book while commanding 2nd battalion, 68th Regiment, W Indies 1800-2, incl a few copies of letters as major of brigade, SW district 1803-4 (1 vol).
British Library (Add MS 45112). Presented by George Chapman 1938.

[153] **HAMILTON, Colonel Henry** (1734-1796)
Lieutenant-governor of Detroit 1776-9, of Quebec 1782-5, of Bermuda 1788-90; governor of Bermuda 1790-4, of Dominica 1794-6.

Journal of his expedition against Fort Vincennes 1778-9 (1 vol); reminiscences 1755-62, written 1792 (1 vol); misc papers (1 box); drawings (1 box).
Houghton Library, Harvard University, Cambridge, Massachusetts (fMS Eng 508, bMS Eng 508.1, fMS Eng 509, fMS Eng 509.2). Acquired 1902 from his great-great-niece Mrs CJ Rice. NRA 20129.

Papers rel to his surrender of Fort Vincennes 1779, incl part of his diary, corresp with Colonel GR Clark, Major-General William Phillips and others 1778-80, and a copy of a narrative of his proceedings 1776-81 (1 vol).
British Library (Add MS 24320). Acquired 1861.

[154] HAMILTON-GORDON, Arthur Charles (1829-1912), 1st Baron Stanmore 1893
Lieutenant-governor of New Brunswick 1861-6; governor of Trinidad 1866-70, of Mauritius 1870-4, of Fiji 1875-80, of New Zealand 1880-2, of Ceylon 1883-90.

Corresp with secretaries of state for the colonies and their officials 1867-90 (4 vols), with colonial governors and administrators 1875-1912 (6 vols), with WE Gladstone, the 1st Earl of Selborne, Samuel Wilberforce and other statesmen and churchmen 1848-1912 (15 vols); general corresp 1841-1912 (10 vols); family corresp 1842-97 (9 vols); letter books 1847-97 (10 vols); misc literary corresp and papers 1852-1912 (3 vols); diaries and journals 1842-91 (17 vols).
British Library (Add MSS 49199-49272). Presented by the 2nd Baron Stanmore 1953. NRA 20961.

Corresp with Samuel Wilberforce 1861-6, and with British chargés d'affaires in the United States 1862-5; general corresp 1861-6; family corresp 1865-6; memoranda 1861-6; diaries 1863-5.
Harriet Irving Library, University of New Brunswick, Fredericton (MG H12a).

Drafts of his despatches, Trinidad 1867-70 (2 vols); manuscript and printed corresp, reports and other papers rel to the administration of Trinidad 1866-71 (5 vols); executive council minutes, memoranda, farewell addresses, etc 1866-70 (1 vol).
New York Public Library.

Drafts and copies of his despatches, Mauritius 1871-3 (2 vols).
Rhodes House Library, Oxford (MSS Ind. Ocn. s.2). Purchased from Bernard Quaritch Ltd 1940.

Letters from WE Gladstone 1851-96 (4 vols).
British Library (Add MSS 44319-22). Returned to Gladstone's family, and presented with the Gladstone papers 1935.

Letters from Lord Selborne 1855-95 (4 vols).
Lambeth Palace Library (MSS 1872-5). Returned to Selborne's family 1916, and presented with the Selborne papers 1962.

Misc corresp incl letters from his father 1844-54, and from statesmen and others 1857-1909, and letters to his nephew the 7th Earl of Aberdeen 1874-1912; commission as lieutenant-governor of New Brunswick 1861.

The Haddo Trustees. Enquiries to NRA (Scotland). NRA 9758 (1/2, 1/4, 1/42, 1/46, 2/64).

[155] HAMILTON-GORDON (formerly **GORDON**), **George** (1784-1860), styled Lord Haddo 1791-1801, 4th Earl of Aberdeen 1801
Secretary of state for war and the colonies 1834-5.

General corresp 1831-41, incl letters rel to British N America 1834-5 (2 vols); copies of colonial corresp 1834-5 (14ff); corresp as prime minister with Sir George Grey 1853-5 (51ff); printed cabinet papers rel to British N American boundaries 1824-46, administration 1834 and fisheries 1854, transportation of convicts to Australia 1852-3, etc (3 vols).
British Library (Add MSS 43197 ff169-219, 43236-7, 43333 ff1-14, 43356-8). Presented by the 1st Marquess of Aberdeen 1932.

See also *Cabinet Ministers.*

[156] HAMILTON-TEMPLE-BLACKWOOD (formerly **BLACKWOOD**), **Frederick Temple** (1826-1902), 5th Baron Dufferin 1841, 1st Earl of Dufferin 1871, 1st Marquess of Dufferin and Ava 1888
Governor-general of Canada 1872-8.

Corresp with secretaries of state for the colonies 1872-8 (12 vols and files); corresp with Alexander Mackenzie 1873-8 (7 vols and files); general Canadian corresp 1872-8 (c20 vols and files); 'private letters received' 1872-8 (20 files); papers rel to British Columbia, the Canadian Pacific Railway, commerce with the United States, etc 1872-8 (2 boxes); papers rel to proposed civic improvements at Quebec c1875 (1 box); letters to the Duke of Argyll 1872-94, Canadian papers 1872-4, domestic account books c1870-80, etc (1 box); press cuttings rel to his tour to Manitoba 1877.
Public Record Office of Northern Ireland (D1071). Deposited by the Marchioness of Dufferin and Ava 1957. NRA 5700.

See also *Diplomats.*

[157] HAMOND, Captain Sir Andrew Snape (1738-1828), 1st Bt 1783
Lieutenant-governor of Nova Scotia 1780-2.

Corresp with Hans Stanley 1776-8 (23 items); letter and order books 1771-80 (3 vols); copies of his letters and orders as lieutenant-governor 1781-2 (1 vol), and c-in-c Halifax station 1781-3 (2 vols); naval journals 1771-3, 1779 (1 vol); account of his service in the American war 1775-7, written 1783-5 (1 vol); memoir of his career to 1794, written c1815 (1 vol).
University of Virginia Library, Charlottesville. Purchased 1939, 1953. *Guide to the naval papers of Sir Andrew Snape Hamond . . . and Sir Graham Eden Hamond . . .*, 1966.

Corresp and papers as comptroller of the Navy
1795-1803, letters from his son GE Hamond 1799-
1806, and misc naval papers of GE Hamond 1824-
62 (1 vol, 230 items).
*William R Perkins Library, Duke University,
Durham, N Carolina.* Purchased 1969. *Guide to the
cataloged collections,* pp226-7.

HAMPTON, Baron, see Pakington.

[158] HANKIN, Captain Philip James
(1836-1923)
Administrator of British Columbia 1869, 1870.

Memoirs 1836-1914; letter to the Duke of
Buckingham 1870.
Provincial Archives of British Columbia, Victoria
(E/B/H19).

[159] HARRIS, George Francis Robert
(1810-1872), 3rd Baron Harris 1845
Lieutenant-governor of Trinidad 1846, governor
1846-54.

Official and personal accounts and bills as governor
of Trinidad, etc 1845-53 (3 files); addresses to him
on leaving Trinidad 1853 (1 file); papers rel to his
wife's jointure 1850, and copies of his will 1852-63
(1 file, 6 items).
Kent AO (U624/A66, O806, T100, T114-15).
Deposited by the 5th Baron Harris 1961. NRA
7617.

[160] HARVEY, Lieutenant-General Sir John
(1778-1852)
Lieutenant-governor of Prince Edward Island 1836-
7, of New Brunswick 1837-41; governor of
Newfoundland 1841-6; lieutenant-governor of Nova
Scotia 1846-52.

Letters to him 1837-41 (5 vols); copies of his letters
to Sir RD Jackson and Lord Sydenham 1839-41 (1
vol); copies of official and personal corresp 1836-40
(4 vols); reports on the Leinster constabulary 1825-
32 (1 vol).
Public Archives of Canada, Ottawa (MG24 A17).
Acquired among the Delancey-Robinson collection
1918, except for one volume presented by
WF Ganong 1934.

Copies of his letters to Lord Durham 1838 (1 vol).
*Harriet Irving Library, University of New
Brunswick, Fredericton* (MG H10 Rep). Acquired
among the papers of Sir SL Tilley.

HASTINGS, Marquess of, see Rawdon-Hastings.

[161] HEAD, Sir Edmund Walker (1805-1868),
8th Bt 1838
Lieutenant-governor of New Brunswick 1847-54;
governor-in-chief of British North America 1854-61.

His papers are reported to have been destroyed by
his descendants (DGG Kerr, *Sir Edmund Head, a
scholarly governor,* Toronto 1954, pviii).

Misc corresp and addresses to him 1853-61 (1 vol);
memoranda rel to confederation 1851-60 (1 vol).
Public Archives of Canada, Ottawa (MG24 A20).

[162] HEAD, Sir Francis Bond (1793-1875), 1st
Bt 1836
Lieutenant-governor of Upper Canada 1835-8.

Letters to him and misc papers 1819-57 (92ff);
letters from him to his uncle Sir JB Burges 1811-22
(41ff); corresp of him and his wife with their son
Francis 1827-72 (7 vols).
Bodleian Library, Oxford (Dep Bland Burges 7
ff115-55, 101-7, 108 ff94-185). Deposited by his
great-granddaughter Mrs FM Morris Davies 1958.
NRA 19920.

Despatch from Lord Glenelg rel to the destruction
of the American steamboat *Caroline,* and copies of
counterstatements forwarded by Head, 1838 (1 vol).
Public Record Office (CO 537/139). Deposited with
the Colonial Office by Head 1869, and transferred
1938.

Letters from Sir John Colborne 1836 and John
Simpson 1837, and misc addresses and replies
1836, 1838 (49pp).
Public Archives of Canada, Ottawa (MG24 A25).
Acquired 1917, 1936.

HEATHFIELD, Baron, see Eliott.

**[163] HELY-HUTCHINSON, Sir Walter
Francis** (1849-1913)
Lieutenant-governor of Malta 1884-9; governor of
the Windward Islands 1889-93, of Natal and
Zululand 1893-1901, of Cape Colony 1901-10.

Most of his personal property is reported to have
been destroyed by fire *c*1912.

Letters to his father 1859-64 (1 bundle); letters
from his brother the 5th Earl of Donoughmore,
with other family corresp, 1864-1901, 1911 (262
items); letters to him and his wife from his brother
Granville 1883-1900 (59 items); corresp with his
nephew the 6th Earl of Donoughmore 1896-1907
(24 items); corresp and notes rel to family history
1904-5 (2 bundles).
Trinity College, Dublin (Donoughmore H/31, J/18-
19, K/10, Y/5-6). Deposited by the 7th Earl of
Donoughmore 1980. NRA 22331.

[164] HERBERT, Henry Howard Molyneux
(1831-1890), styled Viscount Porchester 1833-49,
4th Earl of Carnarvon 1849
Parliamentary under secretary for the colonies
1858-9, secretary of state 1866-7, 1874-8.

Memoranda as under secretary 1858-9 (2 vols);
corresp as colonial secretary with the royal family,

cabinet colleagues, colonial governors and others 1866-7 (26 vols), 1874-8 (48 vols); corresp as member of the Colonial Defence Commission 1879-81 (1 vol); memoranda rel to colonial affairs 1873-7 (3 vols); confidential print and misc papers 1851-89 (77 vols).
Public Record Office (PRO 30/6). Presented by Elizabeth Countess of Carnarvon 1926, and by the 6th Earl of Carnarvon 1952. NRA 20656.

Corresp with the royal family, cabinet colleagues, politicians, the press, friends and others 1850-90 (39 vols); with Colonial Office officials and colonial administrators c1854-90 (12 vols); letter books 1849-85 (17 vols); corresp and papers as under secretary 1858-9 (11 vols); rel to Australia 1862-90 (3 vols), British N America 1862-90 (2 vols), S Africa 1856-89 (3 vols) and other colonies 1866-90 (2 vols); to colonial and home defence 1861-90 (4 vols); to foreign affairs 1864-89 (1 vol); to Ireland 1854-90 (11 vols); to home affairs 1850-90 (16 vols); to the church, incl colonial church matters, 1853-89 (8 vols); to his resignation from the Colonial Office 1878-9 (3 vols); press cuttings and speeches rel to colonial and other issues 1853-90 (16 vols); translations, political and general notes c1851-88 (31 vols); diaries, travel journals and memoranda 1852-90 (49 vols); personal, family, literary and misc papers 19th-20th cent (127 vols).
British Library (Add MSS 60757-61100). Purchased at Sotheby's 24 July 1978, lot 260.

See also *Cabinet Ministers*.

[165] **HERBERT, Sir Robert George Wyndham** (1831-1905)
Assistant under secretary for the colonies 1870-1, permanent under secretary 1871-92.

Letters from statesmen, colonial governors and others 1881-99, mainly rel to his work at the Colonial Office and his retirement, and from CJ Rhodes rel to S Africa 1899 (c80 items).
Queensland Women's Historical Association, Brisbane.

Copies of letters from him mainly to his mother and sister Jane while premier of Queensland 1863-5 (97pp).
Oxley Memorial Library, Brisbane (OM 65-12).

Private corresp with Lord Kimberley and RBD Morier 1880, rel to the Lourenço Marques treaty of 1879 (1 bundle).
Public Record Office (CO 959/4).

[166] **HICKS BEACH, Sir Michael Edward** (1837-1916), 9th Bt 1854, 1st Viscount St Aldwyn 1906, 1st Earl St Aldwyn 1915
Secretary of state for the colonies 1878-80.

Corresp and papers rel to S Africa comprising letters from Sir HBE Frere 1878-80 (96 items), Lady Frere 1878-9 (13 items) and Sir GJ Wolseley 1879-80 (25 items), copies of letters to Frere 1878-80 (3 bundles) and Wolseley 1879-80 (7 items), and parliamentary papers, telegrams, memoranda, etc 1875-1904, mainly rel to the Zulu war and the

dispute with the Transvaal 1878-80 (c60 bundles and items); corresp with colonial governors and officials, memoranda, etc rel to Australia, Canada, Malta and W Africa 1878-80 (7 bundles); letters to him mainly rel to colonial affairs from Lord Carnarvon 1879, 1885-6 (1 bundle), Joseph Chamberlain 1887-1902 (1 bundle), and JA Froude 1875-80 (1 bundle); corresp with Lord Beaconsfield 1869-81 (2 bundles) and Queen Victoria 1877-97 (2 bundles).
Gloucestershire RO (D2455). Deposited by the 2nd Earl St Aldwyn 1969. NRA 3526.

See also *Cabinet Ministers*.

[167] **HILL, Lieutenant-Colonel Sir Stephen John** (1809-1891)
Governor of the Gold Coast 1851-4; lieutenant-governor of Sierra Leone 1854-60; governor of Sierra Leone 1860-2, of the Leeward Islands 1863-9, of Newfoundland 1869-76.

Letter 1874 and memoranda on Newfoundland and on army recruitment nd (1 vol).
Provincial Archives of Newfoundland and Labrador, St John's (P1/8).

[168] **HINCKS, Sir Francis** (1807-1885)
Governor of Barbados and the Windward Islands 1856-61, of British Guiana 1861-9.

Letters from Edward Ellice, Sir EW Head, A-N Morin, James Morris and others mainly rel to Canadian politics and finance 1841-70 (1 vol).
Public Archives of Canada, Ottawa (MG24 B68). Presented by him 1883. *General inventory: manuscripts*, iv, p199.

[169] **HISLOP, General Sir Thomas** (1764-1843), Bt 1813
Lieutenant-governor of Grenada 1803; governor of Trinidad 1803-11.

Family and general corresp and papers, incl material rel to his service in the W Indies, 1783-1842 (1 vol); corresp and papers mainly rel to Deccan Prize case 1813-42 (10 vols); accounts 1803-43 (6 vols); notebooks 1814-34 (7 vols); commissions 1778-1827 (17 items).
National Library of Scotland (MSS 13111-33, Ch 10428, 10437-52). Purchased 1958, 1960 from the 5th Earl of Minto, among the papers of Hislop's wife's family, the Elliots. NRA 10476.

[170] **HOBART, Robert** (1760-1816), styled Lord Hobart 1793-1804, 4th Earl of Buckinghamshire 1804
Secretary of state for war 1801, for war and the colonies 1801-4.

Royal corresp 1801-4 (105 items); letters from cabinet colleagues 1801-4 (c40 items); corresp with Charles Cameron, PF de Meuron, Frederick North and other colonial governors, and reports, statistics,

etc rel to colonial affairs, mainly Ceylon, Malta and W Indies, 1795-1804 (c330 items); patronage corresp 1798-1804 (802 items).
Buckinghamshire RO (D/MH). Deposited by the 8th Earl of Buckinghamshire 1953. NRA 0001.

See also *Cabinet Ministers*.

[171] **HOBSON, Captain William** (1793-1842)
Governor of New Zealand 1840-2.

Journals 1835, 1840, and misc papers 1834-53 (2 vols).
Alexander Turnbull Library, Wellington (qMS and fMS sequences). Presented by his grandson Alexander Rendel 1935.

Letters from him and his wife to Sir George Cockburn, Sir James Graham and others, with copies of petitions from him 1833 and his wife 1843 (19 items).
Alexander Turnbull Library, Wellington (MS Papers 46). Presented by his great-grandson Colonel JM Rendel 1939.

[172] **HOLLIGAN, James Richard** (1820-1869)
President of St Kitts 1864, 1866-7.

Letter book 1866-7.
Rhodes House Library, Oxford (MSS W. Ind. s.14). Presented by Miss MDR Leys 1947.

[173] **HOOD, Vice-Admiral Sir Samuel** (1762-1814), 1st Bt 1809
Joint commissioner to administer Trinidad 1802-3.

Letters from William Fullarton and Sir Thomas Picton, and other corresp and papers rel to Trinidad 1802-5 (149 items); corresp, reports, returns, etc mainly rel to his naval career 1791-1814 (c320 items); letter book 1806-9.
Somerset RO (DD/AH, boxes 52, 60-1). Deposited by Miss EP Acland Hood 1972. NRA 5299.

Corresp and papers as c-in-c E Indies station 1811-14, letter and order books 1794-5, 1806-9, signals and instructions 1790-1, log books 1806-14.
National Maritime Museum (MKH/A). Presented 1952, 1957 by his great-great-great-nephew Commander AA Mackinnon.

[174] **HOPE, George William** (1808-1863)
Parliamentary under secretary for war and the colonies 1841-6.

Political, personal, estate etc corresp and papers of Hope and his family, incl misc material rel to colonial affairs (c237 vols, c1,180 bundles); corresp and papers rel to Colonial Office business, mainly Australia, Canada, New Zealand and the W Indies, incl letters from Lord Stanley and other members of the government, politicians and colonial governors 1841-6 (c80 bundles); to local Scottish and national politics 1835-63 (c20 bundles), constituency matters and parliamentary elections 1834-63 (c60 bundles); personal corresp, accounts, travel diaries etc c1830-63.
Scottish Record Office (GD 364). Deposited 1979. NRA 10172.

[175] **HOPE, John Adrian Louis** (1860-1908), styled Lord Hope 1860-73, 7th Earl of Hopetoun 1873, 1st Marquess of Linlithgow 1902
Governor of Victoria 1889-95; governor-general of Australia 1900-2.

Corresp with secretaries of state for the colonies, colonial governors and Australian statesmen 1889-95, 1900-2 (c175 items); private secretary's corresp 1900-2 (3 bundles); letters from members of the royal family 1887-1901 (2 bundles); addresses to him 1889, 1900-1 (2 bundles); papers rel to celebrations for federation 1901 (23 items); cash books, accounts, etc 1889-94, 1901-2 (10 vols and bundles); photograph albums, sketch books and scrapbooks 1887-95, 1900-2 (9 vols); misc non-Australian political and personal corresp and papers 1882-1906 (11 bundles); commissions and patents 1885-1906 (1 bundle, 10 items).
The Marquess of Linlithgow. Enquiries to NRA (Scotland). NRA 17684. Microfilms of the Australian papers are in the National Library of Australia, Canberra (M936-7, 1154-6, 1584).

HOPETOUN, Earl of, see Hope JAL.

[176] **HOTHAM, Captain Sir Charles** (1804-1855)
Lieutenant-governor of Victoria 1853-5, governor 1855.

Corresp, Victoria 1853-5 (19 items); copies of despatches to and from secretaries of state for the colonies 1854-6 (2 vols); misc memoranda rel to colonial finance, etc, speeches, press cuttings, etc, Victoria 1853-6 (c25 vols, bundles and items); letter and order book as captain of HMS *Gorgon* 1842-6 (1 vol); corresp 1846-55, mainly as commodore, W Africa station 1846-9 (c120 items); letter books, memorandum book, logs and lists of ships and officers, W Africa station 1846-9 (7 vols); misc papers rel to the Argentine Republic 1853-4 (4 items).
Brynmor Jones Library, Hull University (DDHO 10). Transferred in 1974 from the E Riding RO, where they had been deposited by the 7th Baron Hotham in 1954. NRA 5408.

HOWDEN, Baron, see Cradock.

HOWICK, Viscount, see Grey HG.

[177] **HUNTER, Vice-Admiral John** (1737-1821)
Governor of New South Wales 1794-1800.

Journal 1786-91 describing his voyage from England in HMS *Sirius*, settlement and surveys in

New South Wales, and the wreck of the *Sirius* off Norfolk Island (1 vol).
Dixson Library, Sydney (MS 164). Purchased 1918 by Sir William Dixson from Angus & Robertson, booksellers, Sydney, and bequeathed by him 1952.

[178] **HUNTER, Major-General Peter** (1746-1805)
Superintendent of British Honduras 1790-1; lieutenant-governor of Upper Canada 1799-1805.

Civil and military letter books 1799-1805 (2 vols).
Montreal Historical Society. Transcripts are in the Public Archives of Canada (MG24 A6).

Office letter book 1799-1800.
Archives of Ontario, Toronto. See *Guide to the holdings*, ii, p435.

[179] **HUNTLEY, Captain Sir Henry Vere** (1795-1864)
Lieutenant-governor of the Gambia 1839-41, of Prince Edward Island 1841-7.

Misc despatches to him, Gambia 1841, letters to him from his wife and others 1840-59, and corresp and papers of him and his wife rel to his invention of a nautical rigging device 1835-56 (*c*140 items).
Gloucestershire RO (D 48). Deposited by FOJ Huntley 1937-52 and by JFB Huntley 1962. NRA 9215.

[180] **HUSKISSON, William** (1770-1830)
Under secretary for war 1795-1801; secretary of state for war and the colonies 1827-8.

General corresp 1782-1830, incl misc letters from colonial governors, and rel to slavery, colonial trade, etc (26 vols); official and personal papers 1780-1830 (5 vols); papers rel to the French revolution 1792-7 (1 vol), to India 1799-*c*1830 and Ceylon *c*1799-1818 (1 vol), to N America 1805, 1822-8, incl negotiations with the United States concerning boundary questions and W Indian trade (1 vol); speeches and speech notes 1790-1830 (2 vols); accounts rel to the secret service 1795-1808, 1830, and to Cape Colony 1799-1803 (1 vol).
British Library (Add MSS 38734-69, 39948). Purchased 1913, 1920.

Papers rel to NW boundary between the United States and British N America 1824-6 (417pp).
Sterling Memorial Library, Yale University, New Haven, Connecticut.

[181] **IRWIN, Lieutenant-Colonel Frederick Chidley** (1788-1860)
Administrator of Western Australia 1832-3, 1847-8.

13 letters to and from him mainly rel to Australia 1822-49, with other Irwin family papers 1793-1854 (1 vol).
Originals destroyed. Photocopies are in the Public Record Office of Northern Ireland (T2093). NRA 24565.

[182] **JAMESON, Sir Leander Starr** (1853-1917), Bt 1911
Resident commissioner for Mashonaland 1891-4; administrator of Southern Rhodesia 1894-6.

Semi-official letters from JW Colenbrander, King Lobengula, CJ Rhodes and others 1890-4 (11 files).
National Archives of Zimbabwe, Harare (Administrator's Office Records).

Family corresp and papers 1739-1913, incl many letters from him to his brothers 1889-1903 (1 vol, *c*12 items); misc corresp and papers 1890-1919 (61ff).
National Archives of Zimbabwe, Harare (JA 1-2).
Guide to the historical manuscripts in the National Archives of Rhodesia, pp212-17.

[183] **JENKINSON, Charles Cecil Cope** (1784-1851), 3rd Earl of Liverpool 1828
Under secretary for the colonies 1809-10.

Corresp and papers as secretary of legation, Austria 1806-7 (1 file); letter books 1808-10 (4 vols); diary 1809 (1 vol); misc papers mainly rel to the volunteer movement *c*1803-6 (2 files, 4 items).
National Library of Wales (Pitchford Hall MSS). Deposited 1933-4 by his great-grandson Sir CJC Grant.

Letters to him from members of the royal family, statesmen and others *c*1800-51, among corresp and papers of the Jenkinsons and related families *c*1760-1878.
British Library (MS Loan 72). Deposited 1977. NRA 21672.

Corresp mainly 1827-51 (321ff); official and other papers *c*1833-51 (158ff); log book kept while serving on HMS *La Pomone*.
British Library (Add MSS 38303 ff1-273, 38372 ff1-126, 38381 ff1-32, 38475 ff373-407, 38479, 38576 ff135-47). Presented by his great-grandson HB Portman 1911-12.

Letters to him 1808-26 (18 items); personal financial papers 1808-24 (48 items); Bridgnorth election accounts 1812; memorandum of his dispute with Lord Verulam 1827-8.
Mrs Oliver Colthurst (step-granddaughter of Sir CJC Grant). NRA 9005 (286, 289, 329, 331, 446).

[184] **JENKINSON, Robert Banks** (1770-1828), styled Lord Hawkesbury 1796-1808, 2nd Earl of Liverpool 1808
Secretary of state for war and the colonies 1809-12.

Misc corresp with Sir JH Craig, the Duke of Manchester, Sir George Prevost and other colonial governors 1809-12; official accounts 1809-12.
British Library (Add MSS 38243-50 *passim*, 38489D). Presented 1911 by his great-great-nephew HB Portman.

See also *Cabinet Ministers*.

JERSEY, Earl of, see Child-Villiers.

[185] **JERVOIS, Lieutenant-General Sir William Francis Drummond** (1821-1897)
Governor of the Straits Settlements 1875-7, of South Australia 1877-83, of New Zealand 1883-8.

Corresp and papers 1875-83 comprising private letters received (1 vol), despatches and official letters from the Colonial Office and other governors (2 vols), letters and memoranda mainly from S Australian government departments (1 vol), corresp and papers mainly rel to defence (1 vol), corresp rel to patronage (1 vol), telegrams (1 vol), and press cutting books, incl drafts of letters and memoranda (2 vols).
State Library of South Australia Archives Department, Adelaide (GRG 2/20). Deposited among the governor's office records 1968. NRA 27638.

Addresses presented to him 1877-83 (18 items).
State Library of South Australia Archives Department, Adelaide (PRG 124). Presented by Mr & Mrs JW Jervois 1980.

Corresp with statesmen, colonial governors, Australian and New Zealand politicians and others 1875-93 (128 items); family corresp 1877-95 (38 items); copies of corresp mainly rel to his S Australian properties 1885-97 (2 vols); notebook nd; press cuttings 1874-93 (2 vols).
JW Jervois Esq. NRA 27330. Microfilms are in the Institute of Commonwealth Studies, London, and the National Library of Australia, Canberra (M1822-4).

Notes, minutes, etc rel to the political crisis in S Australia 1877 (c8 items).
John Jervois Esq. NRA 27330. A microfilm is in the National Library of Australia (M 1185).

[186] **JOHNSTON, Sir Harry Hamilton** (1858-1927)
Commissioner for British Central Africa 1891-6; special commissioner for Uganda 1899-1901.

Corresp and misc papers 1871-1927, incl letters from FJ Lugard, CJ Rhodes, the 3rd Marquess of Salisbury, HM Stanley and others during his service in British Central Africa (866ff); sketches, Central Africa, Uganda, etc c1880-c1901 (12 vols).
National Archives of Zimbabwe, Harare (JO 1).

See also *Diplomats.*

[187] **KEATS, Admiral Sir Richard Goodwin** (1757-1834)
Governor of Newfoundland 1813-15.

Corresp with the Duke of Clarence 1789-1828 (88 items); letters from Sir James Saumarez and others, and misc papers, mainly rel to his naval career, honours and patronage, 1785-1836 (c105 items); papers as governor of Greenwich Hospital 1822-32 (4 bundles); misc personal and estate corresp and papers 1800-34 (2 bundles, 34 items); autobiographical memoranda to 1811 (12 items); journal of HMS *Superb* 1801.
Somerset RO (DD/CPL). Deposited by Mrs AR Capel 1980. NRA 28066.

Letters from the Duke of Clarence, Lord St Vincent, Sir James Saumarez and other naval officers 1788-1828; papers rel to Greenwich Hospital and the Chatham Chest 1696-19th cent; official service documents nd.
National Maritime Museum (KEA). Presented by Sir James Caird 1946.

Letter book 1809.
Untraced. Francis Edwards' catalogue 1064, 1985, no 342.

[188] **KEITH-FALCONER, Algernon Hawkins Thomond** (1852-1930), styled Lord Inverurie 1852-80, 9th Earl of Kintore 1880
Governor of South Australia 1889-95.

Letters from secretaries of state for the colonies, colonial governors and others mainly 1889-94 (1 bundle); political corresp 1879-89 (5 bundles); letters from members of the royal family 1897-1918 and from the King's private secretary 1903-10 (2 bundles); misc genealogical and other corresp 1895-1907 (4 bundles); log of a river cruise, S Australia 1893 (1 vol); visitors' books, guest lists and household accounts 1889-95, and Sir WCF Robinson's visitors' book 1883-7 (8 vols).
Aberdeen University Library (MSS 3064, 3161). Deposited by the 13th Earl of Kintore 1980, 1984. NRA 10210 (bundles 145, 176-7, 184-6, 190-4, 266, vols 87-95).

[189] **KEMPT, General Sir James** (1764-1854)
Lieutenant-governor of Nova Scotia 1819-29; governor-in-chief of British North America 1828-30.

Letters to him as commander at Kingston, Upper Canada 1814, mainly rel to the attack on Sackett's Harbor (1 vol).
Sir RB Verney Bt.

[190] **KEPPEL, General Sir William** (d 1834)
Governor of Martinique 1796-1802.

Misc corresp and papers 1799-1834, incl a draft of his farewell to the troops on leaving Martinique 1801, and a few papers as governor of Guernsey (c20 items); accounts 1802-33 (5 vols).
Suffolk RO, Ipswich (HA 67). Deposited by the 9th Earl of Albemarle 1955. NRA 4050.

Corresp and papers 1785-1834 rel to a lawsuit between government officials in Guernsey (48ff).
British Library (Add MS 45298, ff270-317). Presented by the 9th Earl of Albemarle 1944.

KIMBERLEY, Earl of, see Wodehouse J.

[191] **KING, Captain Philip Gidley** (1758-1808)
Commandant of Norfolk Island 1788-90, lieutenant-governor 1790-1800; governor of New South Wales 1800-6.

Letter books containing copies of his corresp with the Admiralty, the Colonial Office and other

government departments, and with Arthur Phillip, officials in New South Wales, etc 1788-1808 (9 vols); summary made in 1797 of his letter book 1788-97 (1 vol); corresp and papers rel to Norfolk Island, New South Wales, etc 1783-1807 (2 vols); letters and petitions addressed to him 1794-1807, with other personal and family papers (4 vols); corresp with David Collins and Lord Hobart 1802-6 (1 vol); remarks and journals 1786-90 (3 vols); general order book 1791-6; victualling book 1792-6; schedule of despatches 1800-6; 'Present state of . . . New South Wales' 1806 (1 vol).
Mitchell Library, Sydney (A 1957-8, 1976, 1980, 2015-20, B 54, C 114-15, 186-9, ML MSS 582, 710, Safe 1/16). Acquired by gift and purchase from various sources 1898-1957.

'Present state of . . . Norfolk Island' 1796 (1 vol); notes on signals used in the British fleet 1780-1808 (1 vol).
Dixson Library, Sydney (MS 228, MSQ 522/2). Bequeathed by Sir William Dixson 1952.

Journal 1791-6 (1 vol).
National Library of Australia, Canberra (MS 70).

KINTORE, Earl of, see Keith-Falconer.

[192] KITCHENER, Field-Marshal Horatio Herbert (1850-1916), 1st Baron Kitchener 1898, 1st Viscount Kitchener 1902, 1st Earl Kitchener 1914
Governor-general of the Sudan 1899.

Corresp, Palestine, Cyprus and Zanzibar 1877-86 (41 items); corresp, telegrams, reports, etc, Egypt and Sudan 1884-5 (334 items); corresp with Lords Cromer, Roberts and Wolseley, telegrams, intelligence reports, etc, Sudan 1896-9 (98 items); corresp, memoranda, reports, etc mainly rel to S Africa 1899-1902, India 1902-9 and Egypt 1911-14 (1 vol, c1,175 items); corresp and papers as secretary of state for war 1914-16 (c1,340 items); personal corresp and papers 1884-1916 (c645 items).
Public Record Office (PRO 30/57). Deposited by the 3rd Earl Kitchener 1959. NRA 7283.

Corresp with Lord Curzon and others, memoranda, minutes etc as c-in-c India 1902-9 (52 vols, bundles and items).
India Office Library and Records (MSS Eur D 686). Deposited 1965 by the widow of his military secretary Lord Birdwood. NRA 27457.

Private office papers as secretary of state 1914-16 (23 vols, bundles, etc).
Public Record Office (WO 159).

Misc corresp and papers among those of his aide-de-camp RJ Marker 1898-1912 (4 vols).
British Library (Add MSS 52276-8). Purchased at Sotheby's 22 July 1963, lot 525.

[193] KNATCHBULL-HUGESSEN (formerly **KNATCHBULL**), **Edward Hugessen** (1829-1893), 1st Baron Brabourne 1880

Parliamentary under secretary for the colonies 1871-4.

Letters from WE Gladstone 1860-82 (14 items), Lord Salisbury 1874-90 (13 items), and various correspondents 1832-86 (1 vol); misc letters, drafts and formal papers 1849-80 (16 items); diaries 1849-93 (45 vols); travel journals, Italy 1851 and on a world tour 1887-8 (2 vols); political journals 1857-88, 1890 (12 vols); political anecdotes 1858-81 (1 vol); scrapbooks 1843-92 (6 vols).
Kent AO (U951/C1, 11, 131, 174, 266, F1-3, 25-9; U1963). Deposited by the 7th Baron Brabourne 1962, 1982. NRA 1301.

[194] KNOX, Uchter John Mark (1856-1933), 5th Earl of Ranfurly 1875
Governor of New Zealand 1897-1904.

Official corresp, diaries, press cuttings, etc, mainly New Zealand 1897-1904.
The Earl of Ranfurly.

[195] LABOUCHERE, Henry (1798-1869), Baron Taunton 1859
Parliamentary under secretary for war and the colonies 1839, secretary of state for the colonies 1855-8.

Letters from Sir Francis Hincks 1856-7 (25 items), Sir William Reid 1855-8 (26 items), and Sir HG Ward 1855-8 (50 items).
Rhodes House Library, Oxford (MSS W. Ind. s.36, Medit. s.10, Ind. Ocn. s.126). Acquired 1967.

Corresp and papers rel to Colonial Office business and colonial affairs 1855-8 (c60 items).
Rhodes House Library, Oxford (MS Brit. Emp. s.451). Purchased at Lawrence's of Crewkerne 14 Feb 1980, lot 530.

Letters from Sir John Young 1855-8 (1 vol).
British Library (Add MS 62940). Purchased at Sotheby's 8 Dec 1983, lot 346.

Letters and memoranda from political colleagues and others rel to Vancouver Island 1849-57, and from Queen Victoria and Prince Albert rel to the choice of Ottawa as capital of Canada 1857-8 (98pp).
Public Archives of Canada, Ottawa (MG24 A58). Acquired 1966-76.

[196] LAGDEN, Sir Godfrey Yeatman (1851-1934)
Assistant commissioner for Basutoland 1885-93 (acting resident commissioner 1890, acting commissioner for Swaziland 1892), resident commissioner 1893-1901.

Corresp with Sir GJ Bower, Sir MJ Clarke, Lord Loch and others 1883-1900, copies of his despatches 1892-3, 1896-9, memoranda and other papers mainly rel to Basutoland 1881-1909 (8 files); corresp with Sir Arthur Lawley 1902-8, Lord Milner 1901-4 and Lady Milner 1928-9, and papers

rel to the S African war 1899-1900 and his
commissionership for native affairs in the Transvaal
1901-7 (4 files); corresp and papers rel to *The
Basutos* (1909) and his other publications 1898-1924
(5 files); copies of letters to JA Spender 1901-3
(1 vol); diaries 1877-1934 (61 vols); official diary,
Swaziland 1892 (1 vol); notebooks 1881, 1883
(4 vols); papers rel to appointments and honours,
speeches by him, biographical material, press
cuttings, etc 1866-1957 (11 files).
Rhodes House Library, Oxford (MSS Afr. s.142-
214). Presented by his literary executrix, Miss
D Wilbraham 1959, 1972. NRA 17877.

[197] **LAMBTON, John George** (1792-1840), 1st
Baron Durham 1828, 1st Earl of Durham 1833
Governor-in-chief of British North America 1838.

Official and private corresp with Lord Glenelg and
other members of the British government 1838-9
(12 vols); corresp with the lieutenant-governors in
British N America, the governor of Bermuda and
the British minister at Washington 1837-8 (4 vols);
general corresp 1817-40, mainly British N America
(8 vols); instructions to the lieutenant-governors of
Upper and Lower Canada, New Brunswick and
Prince Edward Island 1838 (4 vols); reports on
political events in the Canadas 1836-8 (3 vols);
papers rel to Canadian defence, political unrest,
immigration, etc 1838-9 (5 vols); addresses, copies
of commissions issued by him, press cuttings, etc
1837-9 (9 vols); engagement diary 1838 (1 vol).
Public Archives of Canada, Ottawa (MG24 A27).
Presented by the 3rd Earl of Durham 1907, 1922.
General inventory: manuscripts, iv, pp146-8; *Report
of the Public Archives for the year 1923*, pp13-410.

Letters from Lords Glenelg, Grey and Melbourne
and others mainly rel to British N America 1837-9
(4 bundles); memorial from the Aborigines
Protection Society 1838 (1 vol); addresses and
petitions to him, with his answers, 1838 (3 rolls,
3 bundles); copies of corresp with Glenelg, of
Charles Buller's sketch of the mission, and of a
printed version of the Durham report (10 vols and
bundles); papers rel to New Zealand 1838 (5 items).
Viscount Lambton. Not open for research in 1985.
NRA 11184.

Corresp with Glenelg, EG Wakefield and others,
and misc papers, rel to the New Zealand Co 1837-
40 (45 items).
Alexander Turnbull Library, Wellington (MS Papers
140). Presented by the 5th Earl of Durham 1940.
NRA 11184.

See also *Cabinet Ministers.*

LANSDOWNE, Marquesses of, see Petty; Petty-
Fitzmaurice.

[198] **LANYON, Colonel Sir William Owen**
(1842-1887)
Lieutenant-governor of Griqualand West 1875-9;
acting administrator of the Transvaal 1879-80,
administrator 1880-1.

Official corresp with Judge JD Barry 1877-8
(2 vols); official letters received 1877-82 (1 vol);
private letters received 1875-81 (1 vol); letters
mainly from him to his father 1871-87 (6 vols);
drafts of official telegrams 1880-1 (1 vol); official
papers 1872-85 (2 vols); diary 1881 (1 vol); MS of
an unfinished novel 1871 (1 vol); printed papers
1877-81 (1 vol).
Transvaal Archives Depot, Pretoria (Acc 596).
Purchased 1956 from CT Wood, to whom they had
been given by a collateral descendant of Lanyon.
NRA 28245.

[199] **LA TROBE, Charles Joseph** (1801-1875)
Superintendent of the Port Phillip District 1839-51;
administrator of Van Diemen's Land 1846-7;
lieutenant-governor of Victoria 1851-4.

Corresp with Sir George Gipps 1839-46 and others
1839-54, memoranda of official corresp 1839-51,
memoranda of his journeys 1839-51, and misc
papers (796 items).
La Trobe Library, Melbourne (H 6944-7639).
Presented by his granddaughter Mme la Baronne de
Blonay 1934, 1952.

Letters and memoranda from Victoria pioneers in
reply to a circular from him asking for information
towards a history of the colony, with related papers,
1853-6 (66 items).
La Trobe Library, Melbourne (MS 10749). Sent by
him in 1872 to the Victoria politician James
Graham for future deposit in a library.

Addresses presented to him 1851, 1854.
La Trobe Library, Melbourne (MS 10106).

Diary 1832-4 (1 vol).
*Thomas Gilcrease Institute of American History and
Art, Tulsa, Oklahoma.*

LAVINGTON, Baron, see Payne.

[200] **LEFROY, General Sir John Henry**
(1817-1890)
Governor of Bermuda 1871-7; administrator of
Tasmania 1880-1.

Letters from Lord Kimberley rel to his
appointments to Bermuda and Tasmania, and from
members of the royal family, statesmen, scientists
and soldiers rel to his military career and his
scientific and literary interests 1844-89,
commissions etc 1831-84, misc printed papers rel to
Tasmania 1880-1, and family and genealogical
papers 17th-20th cent (4 vols, 2 files).
In family possession. NRA 8549.

Letters, commissions etc 17th-19th cent, rel to his
military, scientific and literary interests (5 vols);
addresses from the Tasmanian assembly and
legislative council 1881.
Royal Artillery Institution (MD/1101). Access by
written application.

Journals of a magnetic survey in Hudson's Bay Co territories 1843-4 (2 vols).
Sterling Memorial Library, Yale University, New Haven, Connecticut (Misc MSS 103). Presented by Mrs MT Bingham *c*1970. *National union catalog*, MS 74-1193.

Letters from him to his family and friends, British N America 1843-5 (1 vol).
Public Archives of Canada, Ottawa (MG24 H25). Returned to him, and presented by his grandson Commander PD Crofton 1945.

[201] LEITH, Lieutenant-General Sir James (1763-1816)
Governor of the Leeward Islands 1814-16, of Barbados 1815-16.

Corresp mainly with his military secretary Andrew Leith Hay 1814-16 (4 bundles); instructions, memoranda, petitions, etc, Leeward Islands and Barbados 1814-16 (4 bundles).
Scottish Record Office (GD 225). Deposited by the National Trust for Scotland 1967. NRA 10212.

Corresp and papers 1808-16, mainly rel to the Peninsular war (1 vol, 293 items); misc corresp 1796-1813 (19 items).
John Rylands University Library of Manchester (Eng MS 1307). Purchased at Sotheby's 27 Nov 1961, lot 556. *Handlist of additions to the collection of English manuscripts 1952-1970*, p48.

[202] LE MARCHANT, General Sir John Gaspard (1802-1874)
Governor of Newfoundland 1846-52; lieutenant-governor of Nova Scotia 1852-8; governor of Malta 1858-64.

Corresp rel to raising a foreign legion in N America for service in the Crimea 1855-6 (1 vol).
British Library (Egerton MS 2972). Purchased 1917.

[203] LENNOX, General Charles (1764-1819), 4th Duke of Richmond 1806
Governor-in-chief of British North America 1818-19.

Corresp and papers 1818-19, comprising copies of letters to the Colonial Office and other government departments in London (3 vols), to Sir Peregrine Maitland and heads of departments in the Canadas (3 vols), to Sir Charles Bagot (1 vol), and to misc correspondents (1 vol), general orders (1 vol), abstracts of warrants (2 vols).
Queen's University Archives, Kingston, Ontario. Purchased at Christie's 1969.

Corresp with statesmen, politicians and others mainly rel to British politics and Irish administration 1794-1818 (1,930 items).
National Library of Ireland (MSS 58-75). Purchased from Spink & Co 1930. *Manuscript sources for the history of Irish civilisation*, ed RJ Hayes, iv, Boston 1965, p231.

Corresp and papers as colonel, 35th Regiment 1805-6 (1 bundle); letter books, audience books, addresses, petitions, etc as lord lieutenant of Ireland 1807-13 (14 vols, 6 bundles).
Kent AO (U269/O213-16). Deposited among the papers of Lord Whitworth, his successor as lord lieutenant, by the 4th Baron Sackville 1950. NRA 8575.

Misc corresp and papers mainly rel to his financial affairs 1793-1819 (3 vols, *c*300 items).
West Sussex RO (Goodwood Archives). Deposited by the 9th Duke of Richmond and his solicitors 1965. *The Goodwood estate archives*, ii, pp32-7.

[204] LEVESON-GOWER, Granville George (1815-1891), styled Lord Leveson 1833-46, 2nd Earl Granville 1846
Secretary of state for the colonies 1868-70, 1886.

Corresp with Queen Victoria 1868-70 (1 vol); corresp with cabinet colleagues 1868-74 (17 vols); general corresp 1868-74 (7 vols); cabinet opinions and memoranda 1869-71 (1 vol); corresp, memoranda, etc mainly rel to Colonial Office business 1885-6, incl patronage and the colonial and Indian exhibitions (1 box).
Public Record Office (PRO 30/29/32, 51-68, 71-7, 213). Deposited by his widow 1927 and by the 3rd Earl Granville 1938. NRA 8654.

See also *Cabinet Ministers*.

[205] LIGHT, Francis (1740-1794)
Superintendent of Penang 1786-94.

Letters (in Malay) from Malay rulers and officials *c*1780-1800 (11 vols).
School of Oriental and African Studies, London (MS 40320).

Instructions as superintendent 1786, and corresp with the sultan of Kedah 1790-4 (1 vol).
British Library (Add MS 45271). Presented among papers of Sir TSB Raffles by Mrs MR Drake 1939.

LINCOLNSHIRE, Marquess of, see Carington.

[206] LINDSAY, General Alexander (1752-1825), 6th Earl of Balcarres 1768, 23rd Earl of Crawford 1808
Governor of Jamaica 1794-1801.

Corresp, memoranda, reports, etc rel to Jamaican administration and politics 1795-1812, mainly 1795-1801 (1,267 items), to the Maroon war 1795-6 (267 items), to French émigrés and prisoners of war in Jamaica 1792-1807 (129 items); copies of official corresp 1794-1801 (2 vols); accounts and receipts, Jamaica 1795-1802, and papers 1784-1825 rel to the audit of his official Jamaican accounts (1 vol, 1 bundle, 252 items); military corresp and accounts 1777-1825 (179 items); personal and family corresp and papers 1776-1825 (1 vol, 596 items); British

and Jamaican estate and business papers 1787-1826
(17 vols, 2,190 items).
John Rylands University Library of Manchester
(Crawford Muniments 23). Deposited by the 28th
Earl of Crawford 1946. *Handlist of personal papers
from the muniments of the Earl of Crawford and
Balcarres*, pp24-34.

Misc corresp and papers, Jamaica 1798-1801, incl
copies of corresp with the Duke of Portland and of
memorials from planters, and papers rel to defence
(328ff).
National Army Museum (6807/183/1, ff31-358).
Presented 1968 by the Royal United Service
Institution among the papers of Sir George Nugent.
NRA 20793.

LINLITHGOW, Marquess of, see Hope JAL.

LISGAR, Baron, see Young J.

LIVERPOOL, Earls of, see Jenkinson.

[207] **LOCH, Henry Brougham** (1827-1900), 1st
Baron Loch 1895
Governor of Victoria 1884-9; governor of Cape
Colony and high commissioner for South Africa
1889-95.

Corresp with Sir HW Gordon, Lord Normanby and
others, memoranda and misc papers, Victoria 1879-
93 (4 vols, 8 bundles); corresp with secretaries of
state for the colonies and Colonial Office staff 1889-
96 (*c*27 vols and bundles); corresp with Sir
GJ Bower, Sir WF Hely-Hutchinson, GY Lagden,
JS Moffat, CJ Rhodes, Sir SGA Shippard and
others, telegrams, memoranda, notes, etc, S Africa
1878-9, 1884-1900 (*c*95 bundles); addresses
presented to him, with draft replies, 1891-5 (190
items); typescript copies of corresp and papers,
S Africa 1889-96 (*c*30 bundles); Colonial Office
confidential print, press cuttings and other printed
papers, S Africa 1885-1900 (*c*45 vols and bundles);
corresp and papers rel to India *c*1844-52 (3
bundles), to Lord Elgin's missions to China 1858-
60 and publication of Loch's *Personal narrative of
occurrences during Lord Elgin's second embassy to
China, 1860* (1869) (17 bundles), to his
governorship of the Isle of Man 1863-82
(8 bundles), to decorations awarded to him (2
bundles), and to his personal finances (21 bundles);
general and family corresp 1834-1900 (54 bundles).
Scottish Record Office (GD 268). Deposited by
SD Loch 1971-9.

Illuminated addresses presented to him, Victoria
1885-9 (25 vols).
La Trobe Library, Melbourne (LTEF 923.2945 L 78
A).

Diary of visit to Bechuanaland 1890 (1 vol).
National Archives of Zimbabwe, Harare (LO 3).

[208] **LOFTUS, Lord Augustus William
Frederick Spencer** (1817-1904)
Governor of New South Wales 1879-85.

Copies of despatches to Lord Derby 1882-3 (1 vol).
National Library of Australia, Canberra (MS 589).
Presented by the 3rd Earl of Iddesleigh 1959.

Letters mainly from WB Dalley 1879-86 (26 items).
Mitchell Library, Sydney (A 3057). Acquired 1949.

Letters mainly to him 1848-90, and misc passports
and commissions (82 items).
Edinburgh University Library (Gen. 715/7).
Purchased 1960.

Letters to him and his wife 1853-96 (1 bundle).
Public Record Office (FO 519/284). Presented by his
grandson Sir VAAH Wellesley 1948, 1952. NRA
23469.

See also *Diplomats*.

LONDONDERRY, Marquess of, see Stewart R.

LORNE, Marquess of, see Campbell JDS.

[209] **LOWE, Lieutenant-General Sir Hudson**
(1769-1844)
Administrator of Cephalonia, Ithaca and Santa
Maura 1809-12; governor of St Helena 1815-21, of
Antigua 1823 (did not proceed).

Corresp, letter books, orders, returns, accounts, etc,
Egypt, Portugal, Sicily, Capri, Ionian Islands,
Germany and Netherlands 1797-1815 (37 vols);
official letters from Lord Bathurst, Sir HE Bunbury
and Henry Goulburn 1815-22 (4 vols); corresp with
E India Co directors, military and naval officers,
Napoleon Bonaparte's staff and others, reports of
orderly officers at Longwood, papers rel to
administration of St Helena, Bonaparte's
imprisonment and health, charges against Lowe by
BE O'Meara, etc 1813-29, mainly 1816-21 (51 vols);
letter books and corresp registers 1815-21 (12 vols);
notes of conversations with Bonaparte and his staff
1816-21 (3 vols); misc corresp and papers 1795-
1842 (5 vols); diary 1793 (1 vol); commissions and
appointments of members of the Lowe family 1761-
1862 (1 vol); copies of his official and other corresp
and papers 1794-1822 (27 vols); proof sheets of a
life of Lowe to 1815 by Sir NH Nicolas (1 vol).
British Library (Add MSS 15729, 20107-20240,
29543, 36297 ff12-21, 45517, 49528, 56088-91).
Acquired by gift and purchase 1846-1969.

Corresp, reports, memoranda, notes, etc, St Helena
1815-23 (21 vols, 1 box).
Bibliothèque Nationale, Paris (MSS angl 3-24).

Corresp and memoranda rel to Bonaparte's
imprisonment and the dismissal of O'Meara 1817-
19 (1 box).
India Office Library and Records (MSS Eur E 398).
Purchased at Sotheby's 17 Dec 1981, lot 13.

Corresp and papers 1815-23, incl copies of letters from Bathurst 1815-16 (1 vol), general orders 1816-21 (4 vols), telegraph message books 1819-21 (2 vols), lists of persons landing on St Helena 1819-21 (2 vols), household accounts 1819-21 (1 vol), and papers rel to legal proceedings against O'Meara 1822-3 (2 vols, *c*420pp).
Untraced. Sold at Christie's 8 May 1985, lots 376-8.

18 letters to and from him in grangerised copy of William Forsyth, *History of the captivity of Napoleon at St Helena* (1853) (7 vols).
British Library (Egerton MSS 3714-20). Purchased 1954.

[210] **LOWRY-CORRY, Somerset** (1774-1841), styled Viscount Corry 1797-1802, 2nd Earl Belmore 1802
Governor of Jamaica 1828-32.

Despatches from the Colonial Office 1828-32 (209 items); private corresp with the secretary of state for the colonies and other officials in London 1828-33 (89 items), with Sir Willoughby Cotton and Sir John Keane 1828-33 (156 items), with his secretary William Bulloch 1829-32 (*c*335 items); corresp and papers rel to the Jamaican slave revolt and subsequent trials 1832 (115 items), to the administration of Jamaica and his vindication of his conduct, with a few letters and papers after his return, 1828-34 (*c*170 items), to Irish politics and estate business mainly 1799-1839 (376 items).
Public Record Office of Northern Ireland (D3007/G-H). Deposited by the 8th Earl Belmore 1974. NRA 18797.

[211] **LOWRY-CORRY, Somerset Richard** (1835-1913), styled Viscount Corry 1841-5, 4th Earl Belmore 1845
Governor of New South Wales 1867-72.

Corresp with Sir GF Bowen, the Duke of Buckingham, Lord Canterbury, Sir James Fergusson, Lord Kimberley, Sir Alfred Stephen and others, and misc related papers, New S Wales mainly 1867-74 (620 items); register of private letters 1868-72 (1 vol); addresses presented to him 1870-2 (1 vol); copies of speeches 1869 (1 vol); journal of tour in southern New S Wales 1868 (1 vol); bank book and servants' wages book 1868-72 (2 vols); map of New S Wales and press cuttings 1868-72 (2 vols); MS and proofs of his *Four years in New South Wales* (1904); corresp, journal and day book as parliamentary under secretary for home affairs 1866-7 (2 vols, 93 items); corresp and papers rel to Irish representative peerage elections 1856-*c*1904 (140 items), to the Church of Ireland 1857-1909 (549 items), to the Irish land question 1860-1903 (426 items), to education mainly in Ireland 1872-1904 (191 items), to politics and administration in Co Tyrone 1856-1905 (3 vols, 1,608 items); general political and patronage corresp and papers 1855-1911 (613 items); personal, family, estate and antiquarian corresp and papers 1850-1913 (*c*15 vols, *c*6,300 items).

Public Record Office of Northern Ireland (D3007/J-X). Deposited by the 8th Earl Belmore 1974. NRA 18797.

Letters from his ministers and others, with some draft replies, 1868-72 (2 vols); copies of official corresp 1868-72 (2 vols); misc corresp 1868-72 and papers 1861-73 (1 box).
Mitchell Library, Sydney (A 2542, ML MSS 897). Presented by the 5th Earl Belmore 1946-7 and by the 7th Earl Belmore and his trustees 1950.

[212] **LUDLAM, Thomas** (1775-1810)
Governor of Sierra Leone 1799-1800, 1803-8.

Letters (some copies) to him from Zachary Macaulay, Michael Macmillan and Henry Thornton 1804-9 (30 items).
Brynmor Jones Library, Hull University (DTH/1/2). Presented among the papers of TP Thompson. NRA 10609.

Copy 1808 of his journal of a mission to Sherbro Island 1805 (63pp).
University of Illinois Library, Chicago (Sierra Leone Collection). Acquired 1969-70. NRA 22949.

[213] **LUGARD, Brigadier-General Frederick John Dealtry** (1858-1945), Baron Lugard 1928
Administrator of Uganda 1890-2; commissioner for the Nigerian hinterland 1897; high commissioner for Northern Nigeria 1899-1906; governor of Hong Kong 1907-12; high commissioner for Northern Nigeria and Southern Nigeria 1912-14; governor-general of Nigeria 1914-19.

Corresp and papers rel to his early career 1858-87 (4 vols); corresp, notebooks, press cuttings, etc, Nyasaland 1888-9 (4 vols); corresp with Sir FW de Winton, Sir CB Euan-Smith, EJ Lugard, GS Mackenzie, missionaries and tribal chiefs, reports, treaty papers, notebooks, etc, Uganda 1889-96 (13 vols); corresp with Sir John Kirk 1889-91, 1896-1904 (2 vols); copies of letters from him 1888-92 (10 vols); copies of his official reports 1890-7 (1 vol); misc personal corresp 1888-99 (1 vol); corresp with Sir GDT Goldie, EJ Lugard, the Colonial Office, the British West Charterland Co, etc, reports and memoranda rel to his expeditions to W Africa 1894-5, 1897-8 (4 vols) and to Bechuanaland 1896-7 (3 vols); corresp with the Colonial Office, governors, administrators and tribal chiefs, memoranda, speeches, etc, Nigeria 1900-19 (10 vols); corresp, visitors book, speeches, etc, Hong Kong 1907-12 (4 vols); papers rel to publication of *The rise of our east African empire* (1893), reviews and lecture notes 1892-3 (4 vols); typescript copies of his diaries (originals destroyed) 1889-92, 1895-8 (16 vols), and diaries of EJ Lugard, Nigeria 1903-5, 1912-15 (2 vols); photographs and maps (3 boxes, 2 vols).
Rhodes House Library, Oxford (MSS Brit. Emp. s.30-99). Presented by his brother Major EJ Lugard through Dame Margery Perham. NRA 8555. Some additional papers are reserved from public use until 1995.

[214] **LYGON, William** (1872-1938), styled
Viscount Elmley 1872-91, 7th Earl Beauchamp
1891
Governor of New South Wales 1899-1902.

Letters mainly from governors of other Australian
colonies and their wives rel to federation and the
Commonwealth of Australia bill 1899-1901 (1 vol).
Mitchell Library, Sydney (A 3012).

Visitors' book, illuminated addresses, albums of
views, etc 1899-1900 (63 vols and items).
Mitchell Library, Sydney (A 5016-47, B 1516-27,
D 228-34, *D 290-9). Presented by him 1931.

Diary 1899-1900 (1 vol).
Mitchell Library, Sydney (A 3295). Presented 1951
by David Smyth, to whom he had bequeathed it.

Corresp and papers as lord lieutenant of
Gloucestershire 1911-20 (1 vol, 2 files, 135 items).
Gloucestershire RO (D 551). Presented by the 8th
Earl Beauchamp 1950. NRA 11510.

Scrapbooks of press cuttings, photographs and other
printed material 1891-1938 (20 vols).
Earl Beauchamp. See *Guide to the papers of British
cabinet ministers 1900-1951,* ed C Hazlehurst and
C Woodland, Royal Historical Society 1974, p94.

LYTTON, Baron, see Bulwer-Lytton.

[215] **MACARMICK, General William** (d 1815)
Lieutenant-governor of Cape Breton 1787-1815.

Accounts and corresp with the Treasury 1787-1810
(17 items).
Public Archives of Canada, Ottawa (MG23 F2).
Purchased 1962.

[216] **MACARTHUR, Lieutenant-General Sir
Edward** (1789-1872)
Acting governor of Victoria 1856.

Corresp and papers 1808-66, incl letters to him
1808-61, draft replies, and accounts 1836-56 (1 vol);
corresp and papers rel to emigration to Australia
1836-47 (1 vol); corresp with his parents and
brothers 1810-68 (8 vols); accounts etc 1826-52 and
testamentary papers 1872-82 (2 vols); appointments
1854-66, catalogues of his furniture and library
1854, addresses to him 1856-60, etc (2 bundles).
Mitchell Library, Sydney (A 2899, 2906-7, 2912-19).
Presented 1940 by Major-General JW and Miss
RS Macarthur-Onslow.

Journal of campaigns, Spain and France 1813-14 (1
vol).
British Library (Add MS 44022). Presented by Mrs
AE Campbell 1935.

[217] **MACARTNEY, George** (1737-1806), Baron
Macartney 1776, Viscount Macartney 1792, Earl
Macartney 1794
Governor of Grenada 1775-9, of Cape Colony
1796-8.

Copies of corresp with Lord George Germain 1776-
9 (2 vols); daily registers of official business, Cape
Colony 1797-1800 (2 vols); charts and sketches, S
Africa and S Atlantic islands 1792-8 (2 vols).
British Library (Add MSS 19824-5, 22463-4, 38717-
18). Purchased 1854, 1858, 1913.

Official corresp 1767-1806, mainly with military
and naval officers, W Indies 1778-9 (1 vol); copies
of corresp, proclamations and public papers, Cape
Colony 1797-8 (4 vols).
Rhodes House Library, Oxford (MS W.Ind.s.9; MSS
Afr.t.2-4*). Purchased from Maggs Bros Ltd 1930,
Bernard Quaritch Ltd 1934 and Francis Edwards
Ltd 1937.

Misc corresp and papers, W Indies 1779-95 and
Cape Colony 1797-8 (22 items); misc letters to him,
Cape Colony 1796-8 (*c*30 items).
Public Record Office of Northern Ireland (D572,
D2225). Purchased 1947, and presented by Colonel
JVO Macartney-Filgate 1961. NRA 6465.

Letter books 1777-9 (4 vols); entry book of
proclamations, administrative papers, etc, Caribbee
Islands 1653-1772 (1 vol).
Library of Congress, Washington (Phillipps
Collection). NRA 22523.

Copies of corresp with Admirals Barrington and
Byron and Major-General James Grant 1778-9 (1
vol).
Boston University Library, Massachusetts (Bortman
MSS YZ 1207, F481).

Corresp with Major-General Grant 1779, with
other papers 1774-1807 (32 items).
Boston Public Library, Massachusetts (MS
Eng.461.1-32). Purchased 1972.

Copies of private letters from him to an
unidentified correspondent 1776-9 (1 vol).
Bodleian Library, Oxford (MS Eng.lett.d.373).
Presented by WD Clark 1954. NRA 21249.

Papers 1765, 1776-1800, mainly rel to the war in
W Indies 1778-9, and the administration of his W
Indian estates after his departure (57 items).
*William L Clements Library, University of Michigan,
Ann Arbor.* Purchased 1925.

Proclamations issued by WL Leyborne and William
Young as governors of Grenada 1771-6, with a list
of new commissions issued following Macartney's
arrival 1776.
New York Public Library.

Commonplace book *c*1767-78, incl observations on
Canada and Trinidad.
Huntington Library, San Marino, California (HM
686).

Letters from Robert Brooke 1795-8 (1 vol); copies
of letters to Lord Melville 1795-1806 (2 vols);
notebook 1798-9 (1 vol); 'Account of the Cape of
Good Hope' by Sir JH Craig 1798 (1 vol);
'Sketches of the political and commercial history of
the Cape of Good Hope' by John Bruce 1798 (1
vol).

HF Oppenheimer Esq (Nos 4050 (I-IV), 5324, 6085). Microfilms are in the University of the Witwatersrand (MIC A732-7).

Corresp, letter books, memoranda, returns, etc 1779-1803, mainly Cape Colony 1796-9 (2 vols, 514 items).
University of the Witwatersrand, Johannesburg (A88). Purchased from Francis Edwards Ltd by Dr JG Gubbins 1931, and presented by him 1932. *Historical and literary papers: inventories of collections, 5: Earl Macartney papers.*

Letters mainly to him from John Barrow, Francis Dundas, Acheson Maxwell, John Pringle and others 1798-1804, and misc papers 1795-1800 (2 vols, a few loose items).
Kimberley Public Library, Cape Province. Purchased 1919. NRA 26032.

Official copies of corresp with Egbertus Bergh 1797-8 (6 items); report by Captain George Bridges on the defence of Cape Colony 1798.
Killie Campbell Africana Library, Durban (KCM 55076, 65168-73). NRA 28622.

Corresp and papers 1779-98, incl a few items rel to Cape Colony 1796-8 (158 items).
William R Perkins Library, Duke University, Durham, N Carolina. Purchased at various dates from 1963.

See also *Diplomats*.

[218] **MACAULAY, Zachary** (1768-1838)
Governor of Sierra Leone 1794-5, 1796-9.

Journal letters to Selina Mills and Henry Thornton from Sierra Leone, corresp with his family, Lord Brougham, Thomas Clarkson, James Stephen, William Wilberforce and others, papers rel to Sierra Leone, abolition of the slave trade, the Anti-Slavery Society, etc 1793-1838, and papers of his son-in-law and daughter Sir CE and Lady Trevelyan (1,014 items).
Huntington Library, San Marino, California. Purchased from Maggs Bros Ltd 1952. *Guide to British historical manuscripts*, pp330-2.

[219] **McCALLUM, Colonel Sir Henry Edward** (1852-1919)
Governor of Lagos 1897-8, of Newfoundland 1898-1901, of Natal 1901-7, of Ceylon 1907-13.

Diary as private secretary to Sir WFD Jervois, Straits Settlements 1875 (1 vol).
Brigadier WJ Jervois. A microfilm is in the National Library of Australia, Canberra (M 1184). NRA 27331.

[220] **MacCARTHY, Colonel Sir Charles** (1764-1824)
Governor of Senegal 1811-14, of Sierra Leone 1815-24, of the Gold Coast 1822-4.

Commissions, record of services and misc papers 1786-1822 (20 items).

National Army Museum (6612/10). Presented by FJH Blake 1966. NRA 20814.

[221] **MACDONALD, Lieutenant-Colonel Donald** (d 1804)
Governor of Tobago 1803-4.

Corresp and papers of and rel to him 1786-1807, incl letter book, addresses, orders and proclamations 1803-4.
National Library of Scotland (MSS 3945-7, 3953, 3972, 3981-3, 3985, 3987-8, *passim*). Purchased 1937.

[222] **MACDONELL, Miles** (1767-1828)
Governor of Assiniboia 1811-18.

Corresp and papers 1779-1825, mainly rel to his military service, and as agent for the Red River settlement and governor of Assiniboia, incl letter book 1811-12 (338pp).
Public Archives of Canada, Ottawa (MG19 E4). Presented by the Misses Macdonell of Brockville 1886. *General inventory: manuscripts*, iii, p153.

[223] **MACGREGOR, Sir William** (1846-1919)
Acting governor of Fiji 1885, 1887-8; administrator of British New Guinea 1888-95, lieutenant-governor 1895-9; governor of Lagos 1899-1904, of Newfoundland 1904-9, of Queensland 1909-14.

Corresp and papers c1879-1919, with a few later family papers.
Mitchell Library, Sydney (ML MSS 2819). Purchased from Winifred A Myers (Autographs) Ltd 1975-6.

Diaries 1890-2 (4 vols).
National Library of Australia, Canberra (MS 38). Purchased from Angus & Robertson, booksellers, Sydney 1932.

Notebook kept during his exploration of the Owen Stanley Range 1889.
Mitchell Library, Sydney (B 838). Acquired 1934.

[224] **MACKENZIE, Lieutenant-General Francis Humberston** (1754-1815), Baron Seaforth 1797
Governor of Barbados 1800-6.

Corresp with the Duke of Portland rel to his appointment 1800, and corresp and papers rel to commerce, defence, slavery, patronage, prisoners of war, relations with the legislative assembly, etc Barbados 1801-6 (21 vols, etc); letter books 1801-6 (5 vols); copies of and extracts from letters and papers rel to Barbados 1721-91 (1 vol); household accounts 1801-6 and inventories of his books and plate 1806 (2 vols); letters from Sir Samuel and Lady Hood 1804-14 (1 vol); corresp and papers mainly rel to his military career, Scottish politics and local defence, and his estates in Scotland and Berbice, 1787-1815.

Scottish Record Office (GD 46). Presented by Mr and Mrs FA Stewart-Mackenzie 1954. *List of gifts and deposits*, ii, pp25-32; 'Source list of material relating to West Indies and South America in Scottish Record Office', pp17-20.

[225] **McMINN, Gilbert Rothersdale** (1841-1924)
Administrator of the Northern Territory 1883-4.

Diary kept during construction of Overland Telegraph Line 1870-2; misc papers 1864-1907.
State Library of South Australia Archives Department, Adelaide (565-6).

[226] **MACQUARIE, Major-General Lachlan** (1761-1824)
Governor of New South Wales 1809-21.

Letter books 1793-1820 (11 vols); copies of his letters to Lord Bathurst 1822-3 (1 vol); commission and instructions 1809; memoranda 1808-21 (1 vol); journals 1787-1807, 1810-24 (21 vols); address from settlers on his departure 1821.
Mitchell Library, Sydney (A 768-800). Mainly purchased from Viscountess Strathallan 1914 and from Angus & Robertson, booksellers, Sydney 1917. MH Ellis, *Lachlan Macquarie*, 3rd edn Sydney 1958, pp531-3.

Letter books containing mainly copies of his despatches 1816-21 (2 vols).
Mitchell Library, Sydney (A 3250-1). Acquired from SJ Lamb 1948-9.

Military accounts 1782-6 (1 vol); letters to his uncle Murdoch Maclaine 1784-1804 and to his brother Charles 1818.
Scottish Record Office (GD 174). Deposited 1924, 1931. NRA 21901.

[227] **MACTAVISH, William** (1815-1870)
Governor of Assiniboia 1858-70; acting governor of Rupert's Land 1860-2, governor-in-chief 1864-70.

Corresp with Hudson's Bay Co officials 1865-70 (2 vols).
Provincial Archives of Manitoba, Winnipeg (HBCA D9-10). Deposited among the Hudson's Bay Co archives 1971.

[228] **MAITLAND, General Frederick** (1763-1848)
Lieutenant-governor of Grenada 1805-10, of Dominica 1813-33 (non-resident).

Letters from Sir Thomas Picton 1797-1812 (80 items); corresp, reports, maps, etc rel to his military service in W Indies 1800-5, his governorship of Grenada 1805-10 and the capture of Martinique 1809 (39 items); corresp and papers rel to the campaigns in Sicily and Spain 1811-12 (c330 items); misc corresp and papers 1777-1840, incl commissions 1779-1813, papers rel to his military career 1793-9, and family corresp 1820-2 (2 vols,

102 items); letter books 1800-3, 1805-12 (5 vols); diaries 1790-3 (4 vols); commonplace books 1799-1808, 1810-12, incl journal entries, copies of letters, notes on the Surinam expedition 1804, etc (3 vols); memoirs 1779-1843 and notes on W Indian history since mid 18th cent (4 vols).
National Army Museum (7902-13). Deposited by AR Maitland 1979. NRA 23388.

[229] **MAITLAND, General Sir Peregrine** (1777-1854)
Lieutenant-governor of Upper Canada 1817-28, of Nova Scotia 1828-34; governor of Cape Colony 1843-7.

Letter book containing copies of 31 letters to and from him 1846-8, incl corresp with representatives of churches at Cape Town 1847.
Rhodes House Library, Oxford (MSS Afr. r.2). Purchased c1931.

MAKDOUGALL-BRISBANE, see Brisbane T.

MANCHESTER, Duke of, see Montagu.

[230] **MATHEW** (afterwards **BUCKLEY-MATHEW**) **Sir George Benvenuto** (1807-1879)
Governor of the Bahamas 1844-50.

Copies of his despatches c1844-50 (1 vol).
Glamorgan Archive Service (D/D Mw). Deposited 1968.

See also *Diplomats*.

[231] **MAXSE, Lieutenant-Colonel Sir Henry Fitzhardinge Berkeley** (1832-1883)
Lieutenant-governor of Heligoland 1863-4, governor 1864-81; governor of Newfoundland 1881-3.

Letters to him and his family 1838-90 (1 vol); letters and papers 1854-68 rel to the Crimean war (10 items); letters and papers rel to his debts 1854 (1 bundle).
West Sussex RO (Maxse Papers 59, 175, 180, 411). Deposited by Major and Mrs JH Maxse 1957.

[232] **MAXWELL, Lieutenant-Colonel John** (fl 1767-90)
Governor of the Bahamas 1779-84.

Corresp and papers rel to 27th Regiment 1767-90 (1 bundle); papers while serving at Quebec 1774-7 (1 bundle); corresp and papers rel to financial and patronage matters, Bahamas 1780-2, 1789 (1 bundle); corresp, accounts, legal papers, etc rel to his personal finances, law suits over his wife's property, etc 1775-90 (6 bundles).
Public Record Office of Northern Ireland (D1556/17). NRA 24565.

[233] **MAXWELL, Sir William Edward**
(1846-1897)
Resident in Selangor 1889-92; acting governor of
the Straits Settlements 1893-4; governor of the
Gold Coast 1895-7.

Notes on Perak folklore, anthropology, religion etc
(49ff).
School of Oriental and African Studies, London (MSS
46941, 46943).

[234] **MEADE, Sir Robert Henry** (1835-1898)
Assistant under secretary for the colonies 1871-92,
permanent under secretary 1892-7; delegate at the
Berlin conference 1884-5.

Corresp with secretaries of state for the colonies
and others 1852-97 (55 items); letter book, Berlin
1884-5; visitors' book 1872-97; anecdote books
1878-94 (4 vols); diary 1895-7 (1 vol).
Public Record Office of Northern Ireland (D3044/J).
Deposited by SRJ Meade 1975. NRA 21971.

Letters of condolence from statesmen, colonial
governors, Colonial Office colleagues and others on
the deaths of his wife 1881, his daughter 1897 and
himself 1898 (c330 items).
University College of Swansea (Grenfell MSS L, M).
Deposited by his niece Viscountess Gage 1953.
NRA 26521.

See also *Diplomats*.

MELVILLE, Viscount, see Dundas.

[235] **METCALFE, Sir Charles Theophilus**
(1785-1846), 3rd Bt 1822, Baron Metcalfe 1845
Governor of Jamaica 1839-42; governor-in-chief of
British North America 1843-5.

Many of his papers are reported to have been
destroyed after the death of his son Colonel James
Metcalfe (Edward Thompson, *Life of Charles, Lord
Metcalfe*, 1937, pviii).

Corresp, memoranda, addresses and memorials
1840-4 (4 vols).
Public Archives of Canada, Ottawa (MG24 A33).

Letters mainly to him from Indian administrators
and soldiers 1805-35 (1 vol).
India Office Library and Records (Home
Miscellaneous 738). Purchased at various dates.
Catalogue of the Home Miscellaneous series, pp497-8.

Letters from Lord and Lady William Bentinck
1828-36 (100 items).
Nottingham University Library (Pw Jf 1699-1798).
Deposited with Lord William Bentinck's papers by
the 7th Duke of Portland 1949-68. NRA 7628.

[236] **MILNER, Alfred** (1854-1925), Baron
Milner 1901, Viscount Milner 1902
High commissioner for South Africa 1897-1905;
governor of Cape Colony 1897-1901, of the

Transvaal and the Orange River Colony 1901-5;
secretary of state for the colonies 1918-21.

General corresp 1872-1925, incl letters from
PL Gell, Lords Goschen and Roberts and Sir
FR Wingate (57 vols); papers rel to the Board of
Inland Revenue and the Royal Commission on
Agriculture 1892-7 (2 vols); corresp rel to S Africa
1897-1925, incl letters from Joseph Chamberlain,
Alfred Lyttelton and governors of Natal and Orange
River Colony (61 vols); papers rel to S Africa 1892-
1907, incl Cape, Transvaal and Orange River
affairs, education, railways, the Jameson raid and
Bloemfontein conference (110 vols, 175 items); rel
to the first world war, National Service League,
Ireland etc 1886-1925 (59 vols, 12 boxes and
bundles); as colonial secretary 1918-21, incl corresp
with Lord Buxton, the Duke of Connaught, and
other colonial governors, and papers rel to Egypt
(103 vols, 83 items); command and other official
printed papers, press cuttings etc 1857-1939 (133
vols, 126 items); diaries and notebooks, incl those
of his private secretary Sir HC Thornton, 1875-
1925 (60 vols); personal, family and business
corresp and papers 1824-1928 (38 vols, 37 items).
Bodleian Library, Oxford (MSS Milner Dep. 1-684;
MSS Eng. hist. c.686-709, d.362, e.305-7).
Deposited 1964 by New College to which they had
been presented by Lady Milner in 1933, with
further papers presented by JG Milner in 1973.
NRA 14300.

Addresses presented to him, visitors' books, press
cuttings and other misc corresp and papers 1893-
1955, mainly S Africa 1897-1905 (15 vols, 2
bundles, 249 items).
New College, Oxford. Presented by Lady Milner
1933. FW Steer, *The archives of New College,
Oxford*, 1974, pp106-9.

Corresp and papers as secretary of state for war and
for the colonies 1915-20 (25 pieces).
Public Record Office (PRO 30/30). Presented 1928
by Lady Milner. NRA 23395.

Misc family and other corresp, speeches, notes,
memorabilia etc 1872-1956 (1 vol, 7 bundles, 48
items).
In family possession. NRA 20659.

Corresp rel to Toynbee Hall 1913-23 (30 items).
Greater London RO (A/TOY/6/1-49). Deposited
1967 among the records of Toynbee Hall. NRA
11641.

[237] **MILNES, Sir Robert Shore** (1746-1837),
1st Bt 1801
Governor of Martinique 1795-6; lieutenant-governor
of Lower Canada 1799-1805.

Entry book of despatches rel to crown and clergy
estates, land grants and colonisation in Lower
Canada 1799-1805 (1 vol).
Public Archives of Canada, Ottawa (MG24 A7).
Presented by Lieutenant-Colonel EI Caldwell 1957.

[238] **MILTON, Sir William Henry** (1854-1930)
Acting administrator of Southern Rhodesia 1897-8,
administrator 1898-1914.

Official corresp, telegrams, warrants and press
cuttings *c*1896-1930 (419ff).
National Archives of Zimbabwe, Harare (MI 1).

Corresp rel to diamond fields, native labour, etc
1900-9 (1 file).
National Archives of Zimbabwe, Harare
(Administrator's Office Records).

MINTO, Earls of, see Elliot G; Elliot-Murray-
Kynynmound.

[239] **MOLESWORTH, Sir William** (1810-1855),
8th Bt 1823
Secretary of state for the colonies 1855.

Corresp and papers.
In family possession. Not open for research. See
MG Fawcett, *Life of the Right Hon Sir William
Molesworth, Bart, MP, FRS* (1901).

[240] **MOLONEY, Sir Cornelius Alfred**
(1848-1913)
Acting administrator of Lagos 1878-83
(intermittently); administrator of the Gambia 1884-
6, of Lagos 1886; governor of Lagos 1886-91, of
British Honduras 1891-7, of the Windward Islands
1897-1900, of Trinidad and Tobago 1900-4.

Copies of his despatches to the secretary of state for
the colonies 1894, 1896 (2 vols).
Rhodes House Library, Oxford (MSS W. Ind. s.2-3).
Purchased by the Rhodes Trustees from
IK Fletcher 1930.

[241] **MONCK, Charles Stanley** (1819-1894), 4th
Viscount Monck 1849
Governor-in-chief of British North America 1861-7;
governor-general of Canada 1867-8.

Corresp, memoranda, etc, British N America 1861-
8, incl letters from Sir FWA Bruce, AC Hamilton-
Gordon, Sir JA Macdonald and Sir RG
MacDonnell (*c*185 items); personal, family and
estate corresp and papers 1847-1918 (*c*190 items).
Hon Mrs Batt (his great-granddaughter). NRA
26697.

Corresp and misc papers, British N America 1861-
70, mainly letters from CB Adderley, Edward
Cardwell and Lords Carnarvon and Lyons
(160 items).
National Library of Ireland (MSS 27017-22).
Deposited by Mrs Batt 1976. NRA 26697.

Letters mainly to him and his wife from British,
Irish and Canadian statesmen, authors, churchmen,
etc 1805-89 (2 vols); letters from him to his elder
son 1855-69 (2 vols); draft replies to addresses
1861-8, with a few addresses and petitions received
1862, 1867 (2 vols).

Public Archives of Canada, Ottawa (MG27 IB1).
Presented by the 6th Viscount Monck 1950, and
purchased at Sotheby's 23 Mar 1981, lot 353. NRA
28104.

Diary 1840-4 (1 vol).
In private possession. A photocopy is in the
University of British Columbia Library, Vancouver.

[242] **MONK, Sir James** (1745-1826)
Administrator of Lower Canada 1819-20.

Corresp 1776-1826 (1 vol); notebook 1805-6 (1 vol).
Public Archives of Canada, Ottawa (MG23 GII 19/
2-3). Correspondence presented by JL Russell 1959,
notebook by Birmingham Public Library 1964.

[243] **MONTAGU, William** (1771-1843), styled
Viscount Mandeville 1772-88, 5th Duke of
Manchester 1788
Governor of Jamaica 1808-27.

Letters from the 2nd Earl of Liverpool and the
Duke of Wellington and other political and general
corresp 1793-*c*1830 (7 bundles and items); papers
rel to the remuneration of the governor of Jamaica
1807, etc (1 bundle), to a case 1825-6 concerning
his deportation of a coloured man from Jamaica in
1823 (1 bundle), to his sinecure collectorship of
customs *c*1790 (1 bundle), to the Huntingdonshire
lieutenancy and militia 1743-1800, 1842 (33 items).
Cambridgeshire RO, Huntingdon (ddM 10.6,12-13;
21b.7-8; 26.12; 49.9,11-12,16-18; 85.11-12).
Deposited by the 10th Duke of Manchester 1948,
1954. NRA 0902.

MONTEAGLE OF BRANDON, Baron, see
Rice.

[244] **MOODY, Major-General Richard
Clement** (1813-1887)
Lieutenant-governor of the Falkland Islands 1841-3,
governor 1843-7; lieutenant-governor and chief
commissioner for lands and works of British
Columbia 1858-63.

Letters from Oliver Wells 1859 and Sir JF
Burgoyne 1863; copies of his letters to James
Douglas 1859 (7 vols); letters of appointment 1858.
Provincial Archives of British Columbia, Victoria
(C/AB/30.7J, vols 1-7). Presented 1950 by his
great-nephew, Major RC Lowndes.

[245] **MOSS, Frederick Joseph** (1829-1904)
Resident commissioner for the Cook Islands 1890-8.

Corresp with the New Zealand premier's office
1892-1900 (34 items); general corresp 1868-1905
(96 items); family corresp 1852-1905 (86 items);
papers rel to visit to Mangaia 1891 (1 file); official
papers, Cook Islands 1893 (1 file); papers rel to the
case of Makea Daniela *c*1899 (18 items); misc New
Zealand parliamentary papers 1876-1904; notebooks

*c*1886, 1903 and nd (4 files); MS history of the Pacific; literary and misc papers (36 items); press cuttings, etc (2 files).
Auckland University Library (MSS & Archives A-33). Acquired from the estate of James Rutherford 1963. NRA 27157.

Corresp with CW Banks, Makea Daniela, Lords Glasgow, Onslow and Ranfurly, Sir JB Thurston and others 1876-1904 (*c*1,550pp); constitution of the Cook Islands 1891 (19pp); scrapbooks containing copies of letters, press cuttings, etc (3 vols); misc memoranda, proclamations, etc *c*1890-9.
Auckland Institute and Museum Library (MS 215). NRA 28111.

MULGRAVE, Earl of, see Phipps.

[246] MURRAY, General Sir George (1772-1846)
Administrator of Upper Canada 1815; secretary of state for war and the colonies 1828-30.

Corresp and papers rel to his military career in the Peninsula and France, subsequent political, military and colonial affairs, and the publication of *Marlborough's letters and dispatches* (1845) 1793-1849 (214 vols).
National Library of Scotland (Adv MSS 46.1.1-46.10.2.). Mainly presented in 1925 by the Faculty of Advocates, which had acquired them in 1910.

Letters to his brother and sister describing his military service 1798-1818 (256 items); general corresp 1799-1838 (4 bundles); order book, W Indies 1795-6; commissions and other papers (2 bundles).
National Library of Scotland (Acc 6026). Purchased from Sir WPK Murray Bt 1974. NRA 20932.

Corresp with Sir Herbert Taylor 1811-35, the Duke of Wellington 1824-45 and Sir Robert Peel 1828-46 (3 bundles); misc political and military corresp 1828-45 (1 bundle); private letter book, Ireland 1825-7; memoranda and reports rel to local, coastal and colonial defence 1804-46 (6 bundles); misc military papers 1793-1845 (1 bundle).
Public Record Office (WO 80). Presented by Farrer & Co, solicitors 1942.

[247] MURRAY, John (1730-1809), styled Viscount Fincastle 1752-6, 4th Earl of Dunmore 1756
Governor of New York 1769-70, of Virginia 1770-6, of the Bahamas 1787-96.

Corresp with Lord Shelburne and others and misc papers 1749-1804, incl some items rel to Virginia and the Bahamas (116 items).
Swem Library, College of William and Mary, Williamsburg, Virginia. Presented by the 8th Earl of Dunmore 1940, 1947, except for a few items purchased from HP Kraus 1974. NRA 22219.

[248] MURRAY-MACGREGOR, Major-General Sir Evan John (1785-1841), 2nd Bt 1822
Governor of Dominica 1831-2, of the Leeward Islands 1832-6, of Barbados and Windward Islands 1836-41.

Personal and family corresp and papers 1798-1836, mainly corresp with his father and others while serving in Spain and India 1812-22, and letters, memoranda, etc rel to his chieftaincy of the clan MacGregor 1822-9 (*c*130 bundles); corresp and papers rel to his applications for a post in W Indies 1826-9, and his changes of government 1832, 1836 (2 bundles).
Central Regional Council Archives, Stirling (MacGregor of MacGregor Papers). Deposited by Sir Gregor MacGregor Bt 1983. NRA 19926.

[249] MUSGRAVE, Sir Anthony (1828-1888)
Acting president of Nevis 1860-1; administrator of St Vincent 1861-2, lieutenant-governor 1862-4; governor of Newfoundland 1864-9, of British Columbia 1869-71; lieutenant-governor of Natal 1872-3; governor of South Australia 1873-7, of Jamaica 1877-83, of Queensland 1883-8.

Instructions, addresses, memorials and confidential print, Newfoundland 1862-9; misc letters and papers rel to native policy and relations with the Transvaal and the Zulus, Natal 1872; instructions, addresses and press cuttings, S Australia 1873-7; drafts of despatches and confidential letters, corresp with local officials and others and papers rel to immigrant labour, reorganisation of the judiciary, colonial defence, the case of the schooner *Florence*, etc, Jamaica 1877-83; misc corresp, Queensland 1884-8; corresp with Sir RD Hanson, WS Jevons, Lord Kimberley and others mainly rel to his writings on political economy, with literary MSS and press cuttings, *c*1874-80; misc corresp, etc rel to the formation of the Westminster Review Co 1887; private out-letter book 1868-78.
William R Perkins Library, Duke University, Durham, N Carolina. Acquired from William Musgrave 1963, 1970. NRA 27881.

[250] NAPIER, Lieutenant-General Sir Charles James (1782-1853)
Lieutenant-governor of the Virgin Islands 1812-16 (non-resident); resident in Cephalonia 1822-30.

Corresp and papers, Cephalonia, incl negotiations with Greek nationalists, 1822-30 (3 files); misc corresp and papers rel to his case against Sir Frederick Adam, etc 1830-5 (1 file); corresp, memoranda, etc, India 1842-53 (13 files).
Public Record Office (PRO 30/64). Presented by Mrs FA Adam 1956. NRA 23459.

Letters from him to his secretary JR Colthurst, petitions to him, etc, Cephalonia 1823-31 (58ff).
British Library (Add MS 41063 ff16-73). Presented by the executors of Mrs Georgina Bowen-Colthurst 1923.

General corresp 1800-53 (7 vols); corresp with Lords Dalhousie, Ellenborough, Hardinge and

others, India 1841-51 (4 vols); letter books 1818-25, 1831-49 and nd (17 vols); journals 1810-47 (4 vols); copy of Ionian Islands constitution 1817, with his annotations (1 vol); family corresp c1800-50 (3 vols); notebooks, literary MSS, drawings, etc 1809-52 (7 vols).
British Library (Add MSS 49105-47). Presented by the executors of Miss VB Napier 1956.

Official corresp, reports and returns 1816-50, mainly as commanding officer, Northern District 1839-40, and rel to his service in India 1841-50 (13 vols); general corresp 1802-51 (21 vols); family and personal corresp c1801-1849 (16 vols); misc military and literary papers c1801-1850 (4 vols).
British Library (Add MSS 54510-63). Presented by the Royal United Service Institution 1968.

Family and misc Indian corresp 1800-53 (3 vols); drawings and water colours, Europe and N America (1 vol).
Bodleian Library, Oxford (MSS Eng. lett.c.240-1, d.230, Eng. misc.e.603). Presented by his great-great-nephews WF Bruce and JN Russell 1962-3. NRA 13979.

Letters from Indian tribal chiefs 1842-51 (1 bundle); report by him on the Punjab c1849.
India Office Library and Records (MSS Eur C 123). Presented by his great-great-great-nephew WN Seymour 1950.

[251] **NAPIER, General Sir George Thomas** (1784-1855)
Governor of Cape Colony 1837-43.

Letters from Colonel John Hare 1838-43 (1,420ff); corresp 1838-51 rel to the eastern frontier of Cape Colony and the suspension of Andries Stockenstrom (113ff); general corresp 1815-52 (121ff).
National Archives of Zimbabwe, Harare (NA 1).

Family and general corresp, incl some letters rel to Cape Colony 1837-43 (2 vols).
British Library (Add MSS 49167-8). Presented by the executors of Miss VB Napier 1956.

[252] **NAPIER, Field-Marshal Robert Cornelis** (1810-1890), 1st Baron Napier of Magdala 1868
Governor of Gibraltar 1876-82.

Corresp, memoranda, etc rel to India 1848-77 (36 vols, 4 files), and to the Abyssinian expedition 1867-8 (17 vols, 2 files); corresp rel to Gibraltar's border with Spain, expulsion of Cuban refugees from Gibraltar, etc 1880-2 (3 vols); reports and memoranda rel to fortifications, etc, Gibraltar 1876-82 (2 files); visitors' book 1880-2; memoranda, etc rel to Turkey and Asia 1877-8 (1 vol); letters from the Duke of Cambridge, Lord Salisbury and others 1870-89 (3 files); corresp of him and his wife with the British, Belgian and German royal families 1868-1910 (2 files); corresp with his wife 1848, 1865-83 (c5 files); copies of his letters to the Duke of Cambridge c1869-82 (52 items, 2 files); letter books 1870-2, 1875, 1884-5, 1889-90 (8 vols); letters from him to Sir MA Dillon 1878-9, 1885,

and corresp of Dillon as his military secretary 1868-86 (67 items, 1 file); commissions and appointments 1829-74 (c22 items); notes for speeches, memoranda, etc 1871-84 and nd (3 files); misc corresp and papers 1846-89, incl illuminated addresses and parliamentary votes of thanks (c7 vols and files, c40 items); typescript copies of corresp with the Duke of Cambridge, Sir HBE Frere and others 1864-90 (2 files); printed papers, press cuttings and photographs 1870-88 and nd (13 files and items).
India Office Library and Records (MSS Eur F 114). Deposited by the 5th Baron Napier of Magdala 1962, 1967, 1979. NRA 10012.

[253] **NATHAN, Lieutenant-Colonel Sir Matthew** (1862-1939)
Administrator of Sierra Leone 1899; governor of the Gold Coast 1900-3, of Hong Kong 1903-7, of Natal 1907-9, of Queensland 1920-6.

Corresp and letter books, Sierra Leone 1898-1913 (4 vols), Gold Coast 1900-32 (24 vols), Hong Kong 1902-37 (25 vols), Natal and S Africa 1907-37 (23 vols), Queensland 1920-38 (50 vols); reports, memoranda, speeches, photographs, etc, Sierra Leone 1863-1900 (4 vols), Gold Coast 1898-1907 (5 vols), Hong Kong 1903-7 (4 vols), Natal and S Africa 1900-20 (18 vols), Queensland 1920-38 (20 vols); notebooks 1883-7, 1899-1910, 1920-5 (71 vols); appointments diaries 1899-1903 and visitors' books 1899, 1903-9 (8 vols); corresp and papers rel to his membership of committees on colonial affairs 1919-20, 1926-38 (71 vols).
Rhodes House Library, Oxford (MS Nathan 231-5, 248-406, 494-644, 648-56). Transferred from the Bodleian Library 1961. NRA 8981.

Personal and family corresp 1868-1939 (112 vols); corresp and papers while in the Royal Engineers 1880-98 (29 vols), as a home civil servant 1909-20 (87 vols), and rel to the City of Westminster Health Society 1921-30 (3 vols); speeches 1910-36 and other misc papers (15 vols); diaries 1881-1939 (75 vols); notebooks 1876-81, 1887-93, 1897-9, 1902, 1904, 1929, 1938-9 (26 vols).
Bodleian Library, Oxford (MS Nathan 1-230, 236-47, 407-93, 645-7, 657-71). Presented by EJ Nathan 1961. NRA 8981.

Reports, notes and press cuttings, Queensland 1920-6 (30 items).
Royal Commonwealth Society. Purchased 1965.

[254] **NEPEAN, Sir Evan** (1751-1822), 1st Bt 1802
Permanent under secretary for home affairs 1782-94, for war 1794-5.

Corresp 1780-1820 incl letters from Lord Buckinghamshire 1812-16, Sir JL Caldwell 1812-16 and Mountstuart Elphinstone 1816-20 (2 vols); papers 1792-c1822, incl material rel to the island of St Vincent 1792-6 and Bombay 1801-15 (2 vols).

Mitchell Library, Sydney (ML MSS 66/2-5).
Presented by Mrs Eric Crewdson 1948. NRA
28290.

Letters from William May 1797-8, Lord St Vincent
1793-1803, and Sir WS Smith and others 1796-1801
(2 vols, 2 boxes).
National Maritime Museum (NEP). Purchased at
Sotheby's 1931-72.

Copies of official letters and reports to him as
secretary of the Admiralty 1797-8, mainly rel to the
Irish rebellion (1 vol).
British Library (Add MS 21142). Purchased 1855.

Letters and reports to him as governor of Bombay,
with some draft replies, 1812-19, mainly rel to
suppression of piracy in the Persian Gulf 1817-19.
National Maritime Museum (GOS/14). Purchased by
Sir James Caird from Philip Gosse 1939.

Letters to him and drafts and copies of minutes
1812-20 (325ff).
India Office Library and Records (MSS Eur D 666).
Purchased 1965.

Letters from Lord Buckinghamshire 1812-16
(38ff).
India Office Library and Records (MSS Eur B 325).
Purchased 1978.

Letter book 1817-18.
India Office Library and Records (MSS Eur D
1095). Purchased 1985.

NEWCASTLE, Duke of, see Pelham-Clinton.

[255] **NEWTON, Sir Francis James** (1857-1948)
Acting administrator of British Bechuanaland 1888,
1892, 1894-5; resident commissioner for the
Bechuanaland Protectorate 1895-7; acting governor
of British Honduras 1900.

Corresp with Sir SGA Shippard 1888 (38ff); corresp
as colonial secretary of Southern Rhodesia 1923-4
and as high commissioner in London 1924-30
(2,821ff); misc corresp 1888-1939 (52ff).
National Archives of Zimbabwe, Harare (NE 1).
*Guide to the historical manuscripts in the National
Archives of Rhodesia*, pp348-50.

NORMANBY, Marquess of, see Phipps.

[256] **NORTH, Frederick** (1732-1792), styled
Lord North 1752-90, 2nd Earl of Guilford 1790
Secretary of state for home affairs 1783.

Corresp and papers rel to British politics 1754-88,
mainly 1783-7, incl Cabinet minutes by him rel to
Grenada and the Bahamas 1783 (2 vols); papers rel
to American affairs 1760-84, incl letters and
petitions from loyalists and British officers,
memoranda on the Bahamas and American trade
with India 1775-83 (2 vols); misc papers 1774-
c1783, incl 'Thoughts on the importance of our
colonies in the West Indies . . .' (1 vol).

British Library (Add MSS 61862-4, 61867, 61871).
Purchased 1980 from Mrs KC King.

Letters and notes from George III 1768-83 (over
800 items).
The Royal Archives, Windsor Castle. Presented to
Queen Victoria before 1867, and incorporated in
the papers of George III. Access restricted.

See also *Cabinet Ministers*.

[257] **NORTH, Frederick** (1766-1827), 5th Earl
of Guilford 1817
Governor of Ceylon 1798-1805.

General corresp 1791-1827, incl letters rel to
Corsica, Ceylon and the Ionian Islands (2 bundles,
484 items); corresp and papers, Ceylon 1798-1811,
incl letters from Lord Melville, Lord Wellesley and
Major-General DD Wemyss (156 items); rel to the
University of the Ionian Islands 1817-27 (c3,300
items); personal and official accounts as chamberlain
of the Exchequer 1819-26 (30 items); corresp and
papers of Lord Glenbervie as his attorney 1795-
1814 (c5 bundles, c430 items); misc papers 1794-
1827 (1 roll, 21 items).
Kent AO (U 471). Deposited by the 9th Earl of
Guilford 1954, 1976. NRA 5392.

Corresp and papers, Ceylon 1798-1805 (c80 items).
Untraced. Passed to his executor the 2nd Earl of
Sheffield and sold with other papers from Sheffield
Park at Phillips's 2 July 1981, lot 302.

Copies of his letters to members of his family 1809-
12 (50 items).
British Library (Add MS 61985). Purchased at
Phillips's 2 July 1981, lot 298.

Corresp, letter books, accounts, memoranda and
other papers mainly rel to the University of the
Ionian Islands 1810-27 (c400 vols and items).
Anagnostiki Etairias Kerkyras, Corfu. Purchased at
Phillips's 2 July 1981, lot 299. *Kerkyraiko archeio
Guilford*, Kerkyra 1984.

Copies of letters from him to Lord Bathurst,
Stratford Canning, Sir Richard Church and others
1827 (1 vol).
*Gennadius Library, American School of Classical
Studies, Athens* (MS 108). Purchased 1910 from
PJ Dobell & Son who had acquired it from the
collection of Sir Thomas Phillipps.

Misc papers, incl linguistic notes, plans of the
University of the Ionian Islands etc (1 vol, etc).
Bodleian Library, Oxford (North MSS a.14, b.16
ff327-8). Presented 1932 by the Pilgrim Trust to
which they had been sold by the North family.
NRA 0837.

[258] **NUGENT, Field-Marshal Sir George**
(1757-1849), 1st Bt 1806
Lieutenant-governor of Jamaica 1801-6.

Corresp with statesmen, soldiers and others, and
misc returns, memoranda, etc, Jamaica 1801-6, a
copy of Governor Campbell's memoir on the

defence of the island 1782, and a few papers of
Lord Balcarres 1798-1801 (7 vols); corresp, general
orders, returns and memoranda 1792-1815, mainly
rel to his military commands in England, Ireland
and India (9 vols); maps, plans and sketches,
Ireland and W Indies, and misc papers, c1780-1814
(62 items).
National Army Museum (6807/173-83). Presented to
the Royal United Service Institution by Captain
GGB Nugent 1923, and transferred 1968. NRA
20793.

Corresp with statesmen, soldiers, colonial
administrators and others, despatches from the
Colonial Office and papers 1793-1806, mainly rel to
the revolution in St Domingue, Jamaican commerce
and defence, and British settlement in the bay of
Honduras (c900 items).
Institute of Jamaica, Kingston (MS 72). Presented
by the Royal United Service Institution before
1938. KE Ingram, *Sources of Jamaican history 1655-
1838*, i, 1976, pp360-4.

[259] **OAKES, Lieutenant-General Sir
Hildebrand** (1754-1822), 1st Bt 1813
Civil commissioner for Malta 1810-13.

Letters from Lady Hester Stanhope 1810-17 (25
items), letter from CL Meryon 1811, copy of letter
from Oakes to Lady Hester 1811.
Victoria and Albert Museum Library. Bequeathed by
John Forster 1876. NRA 13466.

[260] **O'BRIEN, Sir George Thomas Michael**
(1844-1906)
Governor of Fiji 1897-1902.

Misc papers, Hong Kong c1892-7, address from
native chiefs and officials in Fiji 1901, and other
corresp and papers rel to honours, personal
expenses, publications etc 1875-1906 (c5 bundles).
Brynmor Jones Library, Hull University (DD LG/
46/18,23;52/76).

[261] **O'CONNELL, Colonel Sir Maurice
Charles** (1812-1879)
Administrator of Queensland 1868, 1871, 1874-5,
1877.

Letters to him and his father Sir MCP O'Connell,
drafts of replies and misc papers 1829-71 (1 vol).
Mitchell Library, Sydney (A 839).

Letters to his father from William Bligh 1816 and
the Foreign Office 1838, letters from him to his
father 1835-8, letters to him and his wife from his
father and others 1838-49, and misc papers (116pp).
In private possession. A microfilm is in the Mitchell
Library, Sydney (FM4/460).

[262] **O'CONNELL, Lieutenant-General Sir
Maurice Charles Philip** (1768-1848)
Lieutenant-governor of New South Wales 1810-14,
acting governor 1846.

See O'Connell MC.

[263] **ONSLOW, William Hillier** (1853-1911),
4th Earl of Onslow 1870
Parliamentary under secretary for the colonies
1887-8, 1900-3; governor of New Zealand 1888-92.

Political and personal corresp and papers 1887-
1903, incl a few papers rel to Australia and New
Zealand 1889-92, and corresp with Austen
Chamberlain, Joseph Chamberlain, Lord Milner
and others, memoranda, reports, etc rel to colonial
affairs 1900-3 (5 vols); political and personal corresp
and papers 1863-87, 1904-11 (11 vols); letters
mainly from political colleagues 1886-1911, with
misc family papers 1635-1862 (2 vols); misc
personal corresp 1900-10 (1 vol); diaries 1869-74,
1878-9, 1884-5, 1889, 1892 (12 vols); travel
journals 1861, 1867-8, 1883-5, 1888-97 (7 vols).
Surrey RO, Guildford (173). Deposited by the
dowager Countess of Onslow 1972. NRA 1088.

[264] **ORDE, Admiral Sir John** (1751-1824), 1st
Bt 1790
Governor of Dominica 1783-93.

Letters from Lord Howe 1793-7, Lord Nelson
1786-1805, Spencer Perceval 1809-11, Lord St
Vincent 1797-8 and others; letter books (5 vols) and
order books (4 vols) 1794-8, 1804-5; signal books
and signal logs 1805 (9 vols); prize accounts 1800-
13.
National Maritime Museum (ORD). Deposited by
Sir SA Campbell-Orde Bt 1967.

[265] **PAKINGTON** (formerly **RUSSELL**), **Sir
John Somerset** (1799-1880), 1st Bt 1846, 1st
Baron Hampton 1874
Secretary of state for war and the colonies 1852.

Letters from Queen Victoria, mainly rel to colonial
affairs, 1852 (14 items); political and general
corresp 1832-79 incl a few letters rel to colonial
affairs (c240 items); letters patent appointing him
secretary of state 1852.
Hereford and Worcester RO, Worcester (705:349).
Deposited by the 5th Baron Hampton 1963, 1966.
NRA 7371.

See also *Cabinet Ministers*.

[266] **PALMER, William Waldegrave**
(1859-1942), styled Viscount Wolmer 1882-95, 2nd
Earl of Selborne 1895
Parliamentary under secretary for the colonies
1895-1900; high commissioner for South Africa
1905-10.

Special corresp with Joseph Chamberlain, Alfred
Milner and others 1882-1941 (12 vols); corresp and
memoranda as Liberal Unionist chief whip 1885-95
(2 vols), as under secretary for the colonies 1895-
1900 (2 vols), as first lord of the Admiralty 1900-5
(39 vols), as high commissioner 1905-10 (with other
S African corresp 1911-41) incl corresp with the
royal family, secretaries and under secretaries for
the colonies, and S African governors and

politicians (25 vols), and rel to domestic politics 1900-14, service in the war cabinet 1915-16, ecclesiastical affairs 1894-1940 etc (20 vols); general corresp 1883-1942 (6 vols); Admiralty papers 1900-5 (34 vols); papers rel to S Africa 1905-10, incl proofs of official corresp with the Colonial Office, lists of addresses presented to him, minutes of meetings of the S African National Convention 1908-9, and diary of a visit to Bechuanaland 1909 (16 vols); family and personal corresp 1867-1942 (29 vols); corresp and papers rel to financial and legal affairs 1883-1945 (22 vols); journals of visits to S Africa 1923, 1930 (2 vols); reminiscences, written 1937 (3 vols); misc personal papers 1880-1942, and typescript copies of letters 1895-1923 (5 vols); official printed papers, pamphlets, press cuttings, etc 1854-1939 (42 vols).
Bodleian Library, Oxford (MSS Selborne, MSS Selborne adds). Presented by the 4th Earl of Selborne 1970-9. NRA 17810, 22802.

Corresp and papers mainly rel to death duties on his father's estate 1881-98, and to trusts on which he and his father served 1883-1932 (41 bundles); corresp of him and his wife with their son Robert *c*1901-1916, and condolences on Robert's death 1916 (42 bundles); personal accounts 1895-1938 (4 vols); pamphlets, press cuttings, etc rel to politics and Hampshire local affairs 1882-1934 (1 vol, 10 bundles).
Hampshire RO (19M75). Presented by the 4th Earl of Selborne 1975. NRA 20787.

Corresp with Lord Gladstone, his successor as high commissioner, 1904-20, and misc official corresp and papers, S Africa 1909-10 (1 vol).
British Library (Add MS 46003). Presented by Viscountess Gladstone 1935.

Corresp with his father 1876-95, and misc letters from members of the royal family 1895-1902 (*c*120ff).
Lambeth Palace Library (MSS 1868-71, 1876, 1879). Presented by the 3rd Earl of Selborne 1962.

PARKINSON-FORTESCUE, see Fortescue.

[267] **PAYNE, Ralph** (1739-1807), Baron Lavington 1795
Governor of the Leeward Islands 1771-5, 1799-1807.

Letters to him rel to French operations in the Caribbean 1805 (11 items); letters from him to his wife 1777-1801, his brother John 1768-95 and others 1762, 1786 and nd (42 items); misc papers (1 bundle).
University of British Columbia Library, Vancouver. Purchased from Francis Edwards Ltd 1966. NRA 27225.

Letters to him and his wife mainly from Lord North 1769-83 (1 bundle).
In private possession. NRA 26045.

Letters from the 2nd Earl of Northington rel to Irish politics 1773-86 (76 items).
National Library of Ireland (MS 888). Purchased at Hodgson's 13 July 1938, lot 273.

[268] **PELHAM-CLINTON, Henry Pelham** (1811-1864), styled Earl of Lincoln 1811-51, 5th Duke of Newcastle 1851
Secretary of state for war and the colonies 1852-4, for the colonies 1859-64.

Corresp with Queen Victoria and Prince Albert 1853-5 (2 vols, 100 items); corresp, letter books and papers rel to colonial affairs 1852-5 (6 vols, 197 items); patronage register 1853-4 (1 vol); index to his official papers 1852-5 (1 vol); corresp and papers rel to British N America 1858-64, incl letters from AC Hamilton-Gordon, Sir EW Head, Lord Monck and other governors, and papers rel to schemes for an intercolonial railway and to the Prince of Wales's tour 1860 (527 items); to Australia and New Zealand 1859-64 (2 vols, 62 items); to other colonies 1858-63 (2 vols, 111 items); to misc Colonial Office business 1859-64 (56 items); copies of letters to governors 1860-4 (4 vols), to the Queen while he accompanied the Prince of Wales in British N America 1860 (1 vol), and to other correspondents 1859-64 (3 vols).
Nottingham University Library (Ne C 9552-9787, 10155-10226, 10885-11653). Deposited by the Trustees of the Will of the 7th Duke of Newcastle 1955, and accepted for the nation in satisfaction of tax 1981. NRA 7411.

Corresp with cabinet colleagues, colonial governors and others rel to colonial appointments, colonial defence, the Ionian Islands, etc mainly 1855-64, letter book 1859-60, journal of the Prince of Wales's tour 1860, memoranda rel to fortifications on Corfu 1863 and British N American railways 1864, and personal and misc corresp and papers 1822-64 (*c*40 vols, bundles, etc).
St Deiniol's Library, Hawarden (Glynne-Gladstone MSS). Deposited among papers of his executor WE Gladstone 1968. Access through Clwyd RO. NRA 14174.

See also *Cabinet Ministers.*

[269] **PERCEVAL, General John Maxwell** (1814-1900)
Administrator of New South Wales 1859.

Corresp with members of his family and others, Mauritius 1837-8, S Africa and Australia 1851-8, Ireland 1875-87 (41 items); diary, Mauritius 1844-5 (1 vol); commissions and appointments 1836-74 (10 items); address from inhabitants of Hobart 1858.
Public Record Office of Northern Ireland (D906). Deposited by Mrs RJ Perceval 1958. NRA 24565.

[270] **PETTY, William** (1737-1805), styled Viscount Fitzmaurice 1753-61, 2nd Earl of Shelburne 1761, 1st Marquess of Lansdowne 1784

First lord of trade 1763; secretary of state for the southern department 1766-8, for home affairs 1782.

His papers were listed in *HMC Third Report*, 1872, pp125-47, *Fifth Report*, 1876, pp215-60, and *Sixth Report*, 1877, pp235-43.

Royal corresp 1766-83 (142 items); corresp with colonial governors, British and foreign politicians, soldiers and others *c*1757-1805 (75 boxes); parliamentary and politicial memoranda and papers 1770-1800 (3 boxes).
The Earl of Shelburne. A microfilm is in the Bodleian Library, Oxford.

Corresp and papers mainly rel to European affairs, but incl some rel to N America, India and N Africa, 1754-69 (42 vols); corresp and papers 1678-1793 rel to colonies in N America and the W Indies (35 vols), W Africa (2 vols), the Mediterranean (2 vols), the Paris peace negotiations 1782-3 (3 vols) and other colonial matters (4 vols); misc cabinet, Treasury and parliamentary papers *c*1760-97 (8 vols).
William L Clements Library, University of Michigan, Ann Arbor. Purchased by Clements prior to their sale at Sotheby's 11 July 1921. *Guide to the manuscript collections*, 1942, pp220-35.

Abstracts and indexes of his political and diplomatic papers by his librarian Samuel Paterson *c*1794-9, incl material rel to the peace of 1763, the American War and the Paris peace negotiations, 1782-3 (8 vols); collection of MSS rel to public finance, foreign policy etc incl a few papers rel to colonial affairs and trade, 16th-18th cent (48 vols).
British Library (Add MSS 24131-8, 30190-237). Purchased 1861, 1876.

See also *Cabinet Ministers.*

[271] **PETTY-FITZMAURICE, Henry Charles Keith** (1845-1927), styled Viscount Clanmaurice 1845-63 and Earl of Kerry 1863-6, 5th Marquess of Lansdowne 1866
Governor-general of Canada 1883-8.

Corresp with Sir JA Macdonald, Lord Sackville, secretaries of state for the colonies and others, with related papers, Canada 1883-9 (8 boxes); letter books 1883-8 (5 vols); fishing diaries and engagement books 1883-8 (9 vols); notes on Canada, India, etc nd (4 vols).
The Earl of Shelburne. A microfilm is in the Public Archives of Canada (MG27 IB6).

Addresses presented to him 1884-8 (*c*14 items).
Public Archives of Canada, Ottawa (MG27 IB6).

See also *Cabinet Ministers.*

[272] **PHILLIPS, William Edward** (fl 1810-26)
Governor of Penang 1810-12, 1816-17, 1819-24.

Corresp, addresses from inhabitants and other papers rel to his appointment to and departure from Penang 1819-26 (*c*40 items).
Royal Commonwealth Society. Deposited by Mrs WE Phillips 1973.

[273] **PHIPPS, Constantine Henry** (1797-1863), styled Viscount Normanby 1812-31, 2nd Earl of Mulgrave 1831, 1st Marquess of Normanby 1838
Governor of Jamaica 1832-4; secretary of state for war and the colonies 1839.

Political and diplomatic corresp and papers.
The Marquess of Normanby.

[274] **PICTON, Lieutenant-General Sir Thomas** (1758-1815)
Military governor of Trinidad 1797-1801, civil governor 1801-2, joint commissioner to administer the government 1802-3.

Drafts and copies of letters and despatches 1799 (1 vol).
British Library (Add MS 36870). Purchased 1903.

[275] **PIPER, Captain John** (1773-1851)
Commandant of Norfolk Island 1804-10.

Corresp and papers, incl private and official letters to him from 1791 rel to family affairs, Norfolk Island and his naval career, with accounts, commissions, etc (3 vols).
Mitchell Library, Sydney (A 254-6).

Corresp and papers 1793-1829, incl letters from William Bligh and Lachlan Macquarie (1 vol).
In private possession. Photocopies are in the Mitchell Library, Sydney (ML MSS 457).

Corresp 1819-31, and plans of Piper and Bulloch family lands at Bathurst.
Mitchell Library, Sydney (ML Doc 1991). Presented by JE Byrnes 1967.

Misc papers 1802-50.
Mitchell Library, Sydney (ML Doc 2962). Acquired from D Piper 1929.

[276] **POMEROY-COLLEY** (formerly **COLLEY**), **Major-General Sir George Pomeroy** (1835-1881)
Governor of Natal and high commissioner for South East Africa 1880-1.

Notebook 1881.
Royal Artillery Institution (MD/229). Presented by Major CC Colley 1951. Access by written application.

[277] **PONSONBY, Major-General Sir Frederick Cavendish** (1783-1837)
Governor of Malta 1826-36.

Copies of letters to RW Hay and others 1827-35 (1 vol).
Rhodes House Library, Oxford (MSS Medit. s.19). Purchased 1972. See G Donaldson, *Handlist of manuscripts in the British Isles relating to Malta* (1950), p12. Other Ponsonby papers noticed in the *Handlist* have not been traced.

[278] **POPE HENNESSY, Sir John** (1834-1891)
Governor of Labuan 1867-71; acting governor of
the West African Settlements 1872-3; governor of
the Bahamas 1873-5, of Barbados and the
Windward Islands 1875-6, of Hong Kong 1876-82,
of Mauritius 1882-9.

General and personal corresp 1860-90, incl letters
from Major-General CG Gordon, Lord George
Gordon-Lennox, colonial governors and Colonial
Office officials, politicians and others (12 bundles);
corresp and papers, incl many copies made for his
biography by James Pope-Hennessy (1964), rel to
Ireland and his parliamentary career 1844-75
(1 bundle), Labuan mainly 1867-72 (12 bundles),
W Africa 1871-6 (6 bundles), the Bahamas and the
Windward Islands mainly 1873-7 (4 bundles), Hong
Kong 1876-82 incl letters from Lord Kimberley
(5 bundles), and Mauritius mainly 1883-91 (15 bundles)
many original letters from colonial administrators,
politicians and friends (15 bundles); further notes,
copies etc rel to his biography interspersed with
original corresp and papers 1856-91 (12 bundles).
Rhodes House Library, Oxford (MSS Brit. Emp.
s.409). Deposited by James Pope-Hennessy 1974.
NRA 17879.

[279] **PORTAL, Sir Gerald Herbert** (1858-1894)
Special commissioner for Uganda 1892-3.

Copies of his letters to Lord Rosebery and others,
Uganda 1893 (2 vols); letters from him to his wife
1893 (124ff); diary 1893 (1 vol).
Rhodes House Library, Oxford (MSS Afr. s.109-11,
113). Presented by Priscilla, Lady Norman 1951.
NRA 19041.

See also *Diplomats*.

PORTLAND, Duke of, see Cavendish-Bentinck.

[280] **POTTINGER, Lieutenant-General Sir
Henry** (1789-1856), 1st Bt 1840
Governor of Hong Kong 1843-4, of Cape Colony
1846-7.

Corresp, China and Hong Kong 1841-4, incl letters
from Sir TJ Cochrane, Sir GC d'Aguilar,
JR Morrison and Sir William Parker (c24 bundles);
indexes of despatches to the Foreign Office 1841-4
(2 vols), to the Colonial Office 1843-4 (1 vol) and of
his letters to Sir William Parker 1841-3 (1 item);
register of letters received 1841-3 (1 vol);
memoranda, reports, ordinances etc, Hong Kong
1840-6 (c6 bundles); accounts and related corresp
with the Board of Trade 1842-6 (c4 bundles);
corresp with Lord Grey 1847-9 (1 bundle); printed
official corresp, Cape Colony 1847-8 and Orange
River Territory 1851 (4 vols); memorandum and
address book 1844-54 (1 vol).
Public Record Office (FO 705). Presented to the
Foreign Office 1950 by his great-granddaughter's
husband Sir Algar Howard. NRA 23471.

See also *Diplomats*.

[281] **PRATT, John Jeffreys** (1759-1840), styled
Viscount Bayham 1786-94, 2nd Earl Camden 1794,
1st Marquess Camden 1812
Secretary of state for war and the colonies 1804-5.

Corresp with George III 1804-5 (53 items), Sir
George Nugent 1804-5 (1 bundle) and Colonel
Charles Stevenson 1804 (1 bundle); corresp mainly
rel to colonial appointments 1804-5 (3 bundles);
copies of letters from him while secretary of state
1805 (1 vol); papers mainly rel to Senegal and
Trinidad 1803-5 (1 bundle); draft letters to
governors, reports, memoranda, etc rel to colonial
affairs, mainly W Indies, 1804-5 (c100 items).
Kent AO (U840/O22-7, 87, 92-6, 131, 210-15, 217-
18). Deposited by the 5th Marquess Camden
1961-2. NRA 8410.

See also *Cabinet Ministers*.

[282] **PRESCOTT, General Robert** (1725-1816)
Governor of Martinique 1793-4; lieutenant-governor
of Lower Canada 1796-7; governor-in-chief of
British North America 1797-1807.

Corresp as c-in-c Leeward Islands 1779-80 (1 vol);
corresp, Martinique 1793-4 (1 vol); letters from the
home secretary 1793-8 (2 vols), from Robert Liston,
British minister to the United States, 1796-9 (1
vol); corresp with British government departments
1796-1801 (1 vol); entry book of incoming letters
1798-9 (1 vol); copies of letters to Liston, Peter
Russell and other correspondents in the Canadas
1796-9 (3 vols); copies of letters from him mainly
rel to conspiracies in Lower Canada 1796-9 (2 vols);
registers and calendars of corresp 1793-9 (3 vols);
corresp, etc, of military secretary's office mainly
1796-9 (12 vols).
Public Archives of Canada, Ottawa (MG23 GII 17,
series 1). *General inventory: manuscripts*, iv, pp64-5.

Military letter book 1796-7, and register of letters
from the Duke of Kent 1796-9 (2 vols).
Montreal Historical Society. Transcripts are in the
Public Archives of Canada (MG23 GII 17, series
2).

[283] **PRESTON, Jenico William Joseph**
(1837-1907), 14th Viscount Gormanston 1876
Governor of the Leeward Islands 1885-7, of British
Guiana 1887-93, of Tasmania 1893-1900.

Corresp mainly with his family 1848-59, 1893-1900
(38 items).
National Library of Ireland (MSS 13762, 15998).
Deposited by the 17th Viscount Gormanston 1964.

[284] **PREVOST, Lieutenant-General Sir
George** (1767-1816), 1st Bt 1805
Governor of St Lucia 1798-1802, of Dominica
1802-7; lieutenant-governor of Nova Scotia 1808-11;
administrator of Lower Canada 1811-12; governor-
in-chief of British North America 1812-15.

Copies of corresp with Sir JC Sherbrooke and other
military and naval commanders and colonial

administrators in British N America and W Indies 1811-14 (3 vols); registers of petitions received and commissions issued 1811-15 (2 vols); copies of warrants and orders for ordnance stores 1811-15 (2 vols).
Metropolitan Toronto Library. Purchased from Lowe Bros Ltd 1946.

RADSTOCK, Baron, see Waldegrave.

[285] **RAMSAY, General George** (1770-1838), styled Lord Ramsay 1770-87, 9th Earl of Dalhousie 1787
Lieutenant-governor of Nova Scotia 1816-19; governor-in-chief of British North America 1819-28.

Corresp, memoranda, returns, etc, British N America, rel to public finance and commerce 1812-28 (*c*125 items), military and naval affairs and relations with the United States 1813-30 (*c*240 items), agriculture, forestry and communications 1815-28 (3 vols, *c*110 items), Indian affairs 1817-28 (58 items), the churches and education 1818-28 (*c*110 items); general corresp, memoranda, etc, British N America 1789-1839, mainly 1816-28, rel to immigration, settlement, patronage, etc, and incl corresp with the Colonial Office 1816-29 (*c*12 vols, *c*1,340 items); personal corresp, accounts, notebooks, etc, British N America 1816-36 (*c*11 vols, *c*145 items); addresses to him 1817-28 (80 items); journals 1816-28 (10 vols); maps, press cuttings and other printed material, British N America 1815-39 (*c*13 vols, *c*100 items); corresp and papers, India 1799-1832, mainly as c-in-c 1829-32 (*c*15 vols, *c*375 bundles and items); corresp, journals and papers rel to his military career 1790-1838, other than in British N America and India (*c*20 vols, *c*370 bundles and items); general personal corresp rel to military, family and estate affairs 1786-1839 (3 vols, 486 items).
Scottish Record Office (GD45). Deposited by the 16th Earl of Dalhousie 1957. NRA 17164.

RANFURLY, Earl of, see Knox.

[286] **RAWDON-HASTINGS** (formerly **RAWDON**), **General Francis** (1754-1826), styled Lord Rawdon 1762-83, 1st Baron Rawdon 1783, 2nd Earl of Moira 1793, 1st Marquess of Hastings 1817
Governor of Malta 1824-6.

Corresp with Sir Frederick Adam, Lord Bathurst, Sir George Don, Sir Frederick Hankey and others 1824-6 (11 bundles); corresp and papers rel to administration, commerce, etc, Malta mainly 1821-6 (7 bundles); papers rel to legal cases and appeals, Malta 1824-6 (5 bundles); petitions addressed to him 1823-6 (3 bundles); commissions and instructions 1824 (1 bundle); misc papers, Malta 1779-1826 (4 bundles).

The Marquess of Bute. Enquiries to NRA (Scotland). NRA 15459 (pp492, 588-95, 606-8, 617).

See also *Cabinet Ministers.*

[287] **RHODES, Colonel Francis William** (1851-1905)
Acting administrator of Southern Rhodesia 1894-5.

Letters received as acting administrator 1894-5 (1 file).
National Archives of Zimbabwe, Harare (Administrator's Office Records).

Diaries, S Africa 1899-1900 (3 vols).
National Army Museum (7812-26). Presented by the executors of Mrs AA Scott-Duff 1978.

[288] **RIALL, General Sir Phineas** (1775-1850)
Lieutenant-governor of Grenada 1816-23.

Copies of official corresp, garrison orders, etc, Grenada 1822-3 (1 vol).
Untraced. Sold at Phillips's 16 June 1983, lot 514.

[289] **RICE, Thomas Spring** (1790-1866), 1st Baron Monteagle of Brandon 1839
Secretary of state for war and the colonies 1834.

Corresp and papers rel to colonial affairs 1831-3 (*c*20 items); letters from Lord Auckland, Sir Herbert Taylor, William IV and others 1834 (*c*275 items); papers rel to colonial and foreign affairs 1834 (*c*50 items); letters from politicians and civil servants rel to emigration from Ireland to Australia 1836-48, letters to his wife from emigrants 1850-3, and misc related papers (*c*300 items); notebook 1834-5.
National Library of Ireland (MSS 566, 13374, 13376-7, 13400). Presented by the 4th Baron Monteagle of Brandon 1935-6.

See also *Cabinet Ministers.*

RICHMOND, Duke of, see Lennox.

RIPON, Earl of, see Robinson FJ.

RIPON, Marquess of, see Robinson GFS.

[290] **ROBERTSON, Lieutenant-General James** (*c*1720-1788)
Governor of New York 1779-83.

Letter book 1780-3; order book 1781-3; letters from him mainly to military commanders in America 1766-85 (17 items); letters to him, with some to his executors, rel to his military, estate and business affairs 1761-1811 (124 items); accounts, vouchers and other papers rel to his service in America and his property in Florida, New York and Philadelphia 1761-86 (127 items); papers rel to claims on his

estate by the Treasury and by his agent Joseph
Page 1776-1817 (142 items).
Scottish Record Office (GD 172). Deposited 1953 by
the 8th Earl of Buckinghamshire among the
Henderson of Fordell papers.

[291] ROBINSON, Frederick John (1782-1859),
1st Viscount Goderich 1827, 1st Earl of Ripon
1833
Secretary of state for war and the colonies 1827,
1830-3.

Applications for colonial appointments and other
corresp rel to colonial affairs 1832 (3 vols); general
corresp to 1842, incl a few letters from colonial
governors (2 vols).
British Library (Add MSS 40862-3, 40878-80).
Presented by the executors of the 2nd Marquess of
Ripon 1923.

Corresp mainly with George IV and cabinet
colleagues 1826-35, some rel to colonial affairs (200
items).
Buckinghamshire RO (D/MH). Presented to his
great-nephew the 7th Earl of Buckinghamshire in
1910 by the executors of the 1st Marquess of
Ripon, and deposited by the 8th Earl of
Buckinghamshire 1953. NRA 0001.

See also *Cabinet Ministers.*

**[292] ROBINSON, General Sir Frederick
Philipse** (1763-1852)
Administrator of Upper Canada 1815; governor of
Tobago 1816-19.

Journals, autobiography and misc corresp and
papers 1777-1814, incl descriptions of campaigns in
W Indies 1794, the Peninsula 1812-14 and
N America 1814 (2 vols).
*Massey Library, Royal Military College of Canada,
Kingston.* Purchased from Francis Edwards Ltd,
which had acquired them from Miss JCB Robinson
at Sotheby's 5 Dec 1955, lot 465A.

Diaries, Spain 1812-13.
Archives of Ontario, Toronto. See *Guide to the
holdings,* ii, p601.

Commissions and letters of appointment 1777-1841,
misc corresp and papers rel to his military service
1803-52, and a narrative of his early career 1844
(145pp).
CP Robinson Esq. A microfilm is in the Public
Archives of Canada (MG24 A4). NRA 25951.

[293] ROBINSON, George Frederick Samuel
(1827-1909), styled Viscount Goderich 1833-59, 3rd
Earl De Grey and 2nd Earl of Ripon 1859, 1st
Marquess of Ripon 1871
Secretary of state for the colonies 1892-5.

Corresp with WE Gladstone 1880-96 and Lord
Rosebery 1886-1908, incl letters rel to colonial
affairs 1892-5 (2 vols); with SC Buxton,
ED Fairfield and Sir RH Meade of the Colonial

Office mainly 1892-6 (6 vols); with Lord Glasgow,
Lord Loch, Sir HW Norman, Lord Rosmead and
other colonial governors 1882-99, mainly 1892-5 (6
vols).
British Library (Add MSS 43515-16, 43553-64).
Presented by the executors of the 2nd Marquess of
Ripon 1923.

See also *Cabinet Ministers.*

**[294] ROBINSON, Sir William Cleaver
Francis** (1834-1897)
President of Montserrat 1862-6; governor of the
Falkland Islands 1866-70; lieutenant-governor of
Prince Edward Island 1870-4; governor of Western
Australia 1874-7, 1880-3, 1890-5, of the Straits
Settlements 1877-9, of South Australia 1882-9;
acting governor of Victoria 1889.

Misc letters, musical scores by him, press cuttings,
etc 1877-91 and nd (15 bundles and items).
Hercules Robinson Esq. A microfilm is in the
JS Battye Library of West Australian History, Perth
(Acc 1894A).

Addresses presented to him, incl 12 as governor of
Western Australia 1875-83.
Untraced. Photocopies of the Western Australian
items are in the JS Battye Library (Acc 3198A).

Visitors' book, S Australia 1883-7.
Aberdeen University Library (MSS 3064). Deposited
among the papers of his successor, Lord Kintore.
NRA 10210 (vol 92).

[295] RODGER, Sir John Pickersgill
(1851-1910)
Acting resident in Selangor 1884-8; resident in
Pahang 1888-96, in Selangor 1896-1902, in Perak
1902-3; governor of the Gold Coast 1903-10.

Corresp and papers, Pahang and Selangor 1886-94
(1 bundle); papers 1904-10, mainly rel to the
S African war and development of the Gold Coast
(1 bundle); letters of introduction, papers rel to
honours, appointments etc 1871-1910 (2 bundles);
personal accounts, family papers and deeds 1885-
1910 (4 vols, 2 bundles); press cuttings (1 bundle).
National Library of Wales. Presented by IJ Morgan
1958-9.

[296] ROWE, Surgeon-Major Sir Samuel
(1835-1888)
Administrator of the Gambia 1875-7; governor of
Sierra Leone and the Gambia 1877-81, 1884-8, of
the Gold Coast 1881-4.

Papers as second-in-command of Sir JH Glover's
Volta expedition 1873-4 (2 vols).
Royal Commonwealth Society. Presented among
Glover's papers by Mrs R Fairfax 1927. NRA
6389.

Misc corresp, petitions to him, press cuttings, etc,
W Africa 1862-4, 1873-88 (25 items).
Leicestershire RO (18 D 33). NRA 6092.

[297] **RUSSELL, Lord John** (1792-1878), 1st Earl
Russell 1861
Secretary of state for war and the colonies 1839-41,
for the colonies 1855.

Political and general corresp 1838-41, incl letters
and memoranda from Lords Durham, Falkland,
Howick, Stanley, Sydenham and others rel to
Durham's mission, the union of the Canadas, the
boundary dispute with the United States, colonial
defence, etc (7 vols); political and general corresp
1855, incl misc letters rel to colonial affairs (6 vols);
letter book as secretary of state 1855.
Public Record Office (PRO 30/22/3A-3E, 4A-4B,
12A-12F, 117). Bequeathed 1942 by his daughter-
in-law Gertrude Russell. NRA 8659.

See also *Cabinet Ministers.*

[298] **RUSSELL, Peter** (1733-1808)
Administrator of Upper Canada 1796-9.

Corresp and accounts rel to government business,
official and personal finances, etc, Upper Canada
1792-1808 (590 items); letter books as administrator
and receiver-general, Upper Canada 1796-1808 (15
vols); misc papers as receiver-general 1791-7 (3
vols); personal bills and receipts 1792-1808 (610
items); journals 1750-6, 1760-1, 1779-82, 1787 (8
vols); narrative and documents rel to the American
war 1775-82 (9 vols); misc papers 1726-75 (15
items).
Metropolitan Toronto Library. Acquired 1951 from
the estate of RWY Baldwin, in whose family they
had remained since the death of Russell's sister.

Family, business and personal corresp and
memoranda of him, his sister and his father 1720-
1811; corresp rel to Indian affairs 1796-8; account
book 1793-1808.
Archives of Ontario, Toronto. See *Guide to the
holdings,* ii, p609.

ST ALDWYN, Earl, see Hicks Beach.

[299] **SCRATCHLEY, Major-General Sir Peter
Henry** (1835-1885)
Commissioner for British New Guinea 1884-5.

Journals 1855-85 (7 vols, 2 files); reports,
memoranda, sketches, press cuttings, etc, mainly
India, Australia and New Guinea 1854-85 (2 vols, 5
files); personal accounts 1864-72 (1 vol).
In family possession. Not open for research.
NRA 24189.

SEAFORTH, Baron, see Mackenzie.

SEATON, Baron, see Colborne.

SELBORNE, Earl of, see Palmer.

[300] **SEYMOUR** (formerly **CONWAY**), **Vice-
Admiral Lord Hugh** (1759-1801)
Governor of Curaçao 1800.

Naval logs 1773-1801 (8 vols); naval journals,
notebooks and signal books 1782-1800 (13 vols);
orders received 1778-1800 (2 bundles); draft letters
and orders to officers under his command c1790-
1801 (2 bundles); letters from Lord Spencer 1794-8
(1 bundle); corresp and papers rel to a proposed
expedition against Spanish America 1796 (1
bundle); papers rel to British coastal defence and
the Spithead mutiny 1797 (3 bundles); corresp,
intelligence reports, etc as c-in-c Jamaica station
1799-1801, and rel to the expeditions against
Surinam 1799 and Curaçao 1800 (1 vol, 6 bundles);
commissions 1776-1800, misc naval papers c1780-
1802, misc personal corresp and papers 1782-98 (7
bundles, 80 items); travel journals, Morocco c1777-
8 and Europe 1785 (2 vols).
Warwick County RO (CR 114A, 713). Deposited by
the 8th Marquess of Hertford 1951, 1961. NRA
8482.

[301] **SHAW-LEFEVRE, Sir John George**
(1797-1879)
Parliamentary under secretary for war and the
colonies 1833-4.

Letters to him as a poor law commissioner 1834-41
(c150 items); corresp with Colonel Robert Torrens
and others rel to the S Australia commission 1835-
41 (29 items); corresp, reports, etc rel to Board of
Trade business 1842-8, incl memoranda rel to the
Bahamas, Bermuda and Jamaica acts (c120 items);
misc corresp and papers rel to London University
1836-41, the Royal Scottish Academy 1846-8, the
Cambridge University election 1847 and the
Parliament Office 1845-70; misc family corresp and
papers 1827-57; corresp, letter books, memoranda,
accounts etc as auditor of the Spencer estates and
rel to his father's manor of Burley, Hants 18th-19th
cent.
House of Lords RO (Shaw-Lefevre Papers). Left by
him in the Parliament Office on his retirement
1875. NRA 28247.

[302] **SHEE, Sir George** (1754-1825), 1st Bt 1794
Under secretary for the colonies 1806-7.

Letters from the 2nd Earl of Chichester 1796-1814,
the Duke of Gloucester 1805-10, and the Duke of
York 1806-7 (1 vol); corresp as an E India Co
official 1775-87 (1 vol); general corresp 1771-1823,
incl a few letters 1806-7, and misc Indian papers
1780-2 (1 vol).
British Library (Add MSS 60337-9). Purchased
from his great-great-great-nephew Richard Neall
1978. NRA 19146.

SHELBURNE, Earl of, see Petty.

[303] **SHEPSTONE, Sir Theophilus** (1817-1893)
Administrator of the Transvaal 1877-9.

Letters to him 1835-93, mainly as administrator 1877-9 and rel to church affairs in Natal 1883-93 (53 vols); drafts and copies of his official and private letters 1847-93 (12 vols); draft memoranda and copies of minutes 1843-92 (6 vols); diaries 1835-93 (13 vols); misc personal, literary, estate and church papers 19th cent (10 vols).
Natal Archives Depot, Pietermaritzburg (A 96). NRA 28118.

Misc corresp, memoranda, condolences on his death, press cuttings, etc 1838-93 (*c*60 bundles and items).
Killie Campbell Africana Library, Durban (Shepstone Papers). NRA 28622.

[304] SHERBROOKE, General Sir John Coape (1764-1830)
Lieutenant-governor of Nova Scotia 1811-16; governor-in-chief of British North America 1816-18.

Corresp 1813-30 (1 vol); military papers *c*1811-18 (1 vol); addresses to him and his replies 1814-18 (1 vol); journals 1809-18 (5 vols); account book 1809-19.
In family possession. A microfilm is in the Public Archives of Canada (MG24 A57).

Corresp 1811-18 (2 vols); military letter book 1815-16 and register of despatches from Lord Bathurst 1816-18 (1 vol); farewell address from the inhabitants of Quebec 1818, and a few proclamations issued by him (1 vol).
Public Archives of Canada, Ottawa (MG24 A57). Presented by Miss TC Oates 1970-1.

[305] SHIPPARD, Sir Sidney Godolphin Alexander (1837-1902)
Administrator of British Bechuanaland 1885-91; resident commissioner for the Bechuanaland Protectorate 1891-5.

Letters from CJ Rhodes 1886-94 (10 items); draft letter to Rhodes 1894.
National Archives of Zimbabwe, Harare (RH 1/1/1). Purchased at Sotheby's 5 Dec 1955, lot 490.

[306] SIMCOE, Lieutenant-General John Graves (1752-1806)
Lieutenant-governor of Upper Canada 1791-6; governor of St Domingue 1796-7.

Corresp and papers, America and Canada 1762-1807; letter books, mainly Upper Canada (39 vols); corresp and plans rel to defence of SW England 1803; family papers 1665-1834, incl corresp, diaries and sketch books of his wife.
Archives of Ontario, Toronto. Transferred in 1952 from the University of Toronto Library, to which they had been presented by RS McLaughlin 1946.
Guide to the holdings, ii, p624.

Misc corresp and papers, Upper Canada 1791-6 (*c*35 items); letter book 1795-6; corresp 1796-7 and memoranda and other papers rel to St Domingue 1765-97 (50 items); copies of despatches and letters

to and from Henry Dundas, the Duke of Portland and others 1796-7 (3 vols); letter book 1796-1806, incl some original letters and drawings; corresp and papers mainly rel to military affairs 1776-1805 (*c*40 items).
Devon RO (1038M). Deposited 1961. NRA 12870.

Corresp with Sir Henry Clinton, George Hammond and other soldiers, colonial officials, etc, and misc papers, mainly rel to the American war and Upper Canada, 1774-1824 (3 vols); copies of letters from him 1792-3 (1 vol); notebook 1774-5.
William L Clements Library, University of Michigan, Ann Arbor. Purchased from Maggs Bros 1922, 1933. *Guide to the English manuscripts,* 1942, pp235-6.

Letter book 1791-3; draft of sections of his *Journal of the operations of the Queen's Rangers* (1787).
Huntington Library, San Marino, California.

[307] SIMPSON, Sir George (*c*1786-1860)
Governor of the northern department of Rupert's Land 1821-6, governor-in-chief of Rupert's Land 1826-60.

Letters to him 1821-60 (52 vols); copies of letters to him 1821-35 (12 vols), of official letters from him 1821-60 (82 vols), of private letters from him 1853-60 (3 vols), of reports to the Hudson's Bay Co 1822-43 (28 vols); draft letters and shorthand notes 1830-59 (3 vols); misc personal corresp and papers 1841-63 (3 vols); travel journals 1821-41 (6 vols).
Provincial Archives of Manitoba, Winnipeg (HBCA D3-6). Deposited among the Hudson's Bay Co archives 1971.

[308] SKELTON, Lieutenant-General John (1764-1841)
Lieutenant-governor of St Helena 1813-16.

Letters from his family 1795-1824 (1 bundle); corresp of him and his wife with Lord Bathurst and supporters of Napoleon Bonaparte 1816-22 (1 bundle); personal and genealogical corresp and papers 1799-1841 (6 bundles); copies of corresp mainly with his brother Philip and rel to Philip's property 1815-27 (1 vol); journals of voyages to England from Bombay 1810 and St Helena 1816 (2 vols); military commissions 1813-37 (5 items).
India Office Library and Records (MSS Eur E 334). Deposited by Miss PM Powell 1974. NRA 27499.

SLIGO, Marquess of, see Browne HP.

[309] SMITH, Lieutenant-Colonel Sir Gerard (1839-1920)
Governor of Western Australia 1895-1900.

Diary 1895-6, 1899 (1 vol); addresses to him 1895-7, nd (16 items).
JS Battye Library of West Australian History, Perth (Acc 995A). Deposited by GH Smith 1961. NRA 27208.

[310] **SMITH, Lieutenant-General Sir Harry George Wakelyn** (1787-1860), Bt 1846
Governor of Cape Colony 1847-52.

Corresp 1813-46, record of services 1805 and diary of Montevideo expedition 1806-7 (1 vol); corresp 1838-42 and memoranda 1835-6 (1 vol); letter book 1851.
Public Record Office (WO 135). Presented 1941 by his great-nieces the Misses Moore-Smith.

Corresp with soldiers, colonial administrators and others, and misc papers, incl some typescript copies, 1834-1902, mainly rel to Cape Colony and the Kaffir war 1847-52 (*c*290 items).
Cory Library for Historical Research, Rhodes University, Grahamstown (MSS 481-735, PR 28-63). Presented to the Public Record Office 1941, and transferred 1947.

MS autobiography written in 1846.
Cambridge University Library (Add 7036).

Copies of letters from him to subordinates, in the hand of his aide-de-camp Major EA Holdich, 1850-1 (1 vol).
National Army Museum (6807-352). Presented by the Royal United Service Institution 1968. NRA 18641.

[311] **SOUTHEY, Sir Richard** (1808-1901)
Lieutenant-governor of Griqualand West 1872-5.

Semi-official letters and papers to him 1835-72, mainly as acting colonial secretary of Cape Colony 1860-2 and colonial secretary 1864-72 (47 vols); drafts and copies of semi-official letters and papers from him mainly 1860-72 (12 vols); personal corresp and papers 1839-1900 (4 vols); misc letters and papers 1834-98 (5 vols).
Cape Archives Depot, Cape Town (A 611). NRA 28120.

Semi-official letters to him 1872-81 (5 vols); drafts and copies of semi-official letters from him 1872-5 (11 vols).
Cape Archives Depot, Cape Town (GLW 175-90). NRA 28120.

[312] **STANHOPE, Edward** (1840-1893)
Secretary of state for the colonies 1886-7.

Corresp with Queen Victoria and Sir HF Ponsonby 1886-92 (4 bundles); letters from Lords Carnarvon and Dufferin, Sir AE Havelock, Sir RGW Herbert, Lords Knutsford and Lansdowne, Sir HGR Robinson and other colonial governors mainly 1886-92 (10 bundles); papers rel to southern and central Africa 1884-91 (8 bundles), to Australia, Borneo and the Pacific 1886-9 (2 bundles), to the Newfoundland and Behring Sea fisheries 1886-91 (2 bundles), to imperial defence, sugar bounties, etc 1886-91 (1 bundle), and to the W Indies 1891 (1 bundle).
Kent AO (U1590/O239, 243-50, 264, 274, 286, 288, 292-3, 306, 321-2). Deposited by the

Administrative Trustees of the Chevening Estate 1971. NRA 25095.

See also *Cabinet Ministers.*

[313] **STANLEY, Edward George Geoffrey Smith-** (1799-1869), styled Lord Stanley 1834-51, 14th Earl of Derby 1851
Under secretary for war and the colonies 1827-8, secretary of state 1833-4, 1841-5.

Special corresp 1822-69 (50 boxes); general corresp 1826-69 (62 boxes); letter books 1826-69 (33 boxes); corresp and papers, mainly Africa, Australia, Canada, Ceylon, New Zealand, W Indies 1833-4, 1841-5, incl material rel to the colonial church, slavery, indentured labour, convict transportation, garrisons, boundary disputes etc (*c*20 boxes).
Liverpool RO (920 Der 14). Deposited by the 18th Earl of Derby 1980, 1984. NRA 20084.

Despatches from Sir CT Metcalfe 1843-5 (1 bundle).
The Earl of Derby. Enquiries to the Librarian, The Estate Office, Knowsley, Prescot, Merseyside L34 4AG. Access restricted.

Letters and despatches, mainly copies, from Sir Charles Bagot 1842 (1 vol); letters, memoranda and despatches to and from Sir CT Metcalfe 1843-5 (3 vols).
Public Record Office (CO 537/140-3). Transferred from the Colonial Office 1938.

See also *Cabinet Ministers.*

[314] **STANLEY, Edward Henry** (1826-1893), styled Lord Stanley 1851-69, 15th Earl of Derby 1869
Secretary of state for the colonies 1858, 1882-5.

Corresp 1858-9 (1 vol, 339 bundles); notes and papers on colonial and other issues 1858-9 (2 vols); corresp 1882-5 (713 bundles); Colonial Office memoranda and misc papers 1882-5 (2 bundles); printed papers rel to foreign and colonial affairs 1824, 1882-5 (11 vols, 1 box, 9 bundles); diaries 1858, 1882-5 (5 vols); misc speeches, press cuttings etc.
Liverpool RO (920 Der 15). Deposited by the 18th Earl of Derby 1968, 1980. NRA 20761.

See also *Cabinet Ministers.*

[315] **STANLEY, Frederick Arthur** (1841-1908), 1st Baron Stanley of Preston 1886, 16th Earl of Derby 1893
Secretary of state for the colonies 1885-6; governor-general of Canada 1888-93.

Letters received mainly rel to his appointments, but incl a few as colonial secretary, 1869-89 (115 items); corresp, Canada 1888-93, incl letters from Lord Knutsford, Sir JA Macdonald and other Canadian politicians, Sir Julian Pauncefote, Lords Ripon and Salisbury, and WH Smith (393 items).

Corpus Christi College, Cambridge. Deposited by his great-grandson RF Hobbs 1969. NRA 11916.

Misc papers, mainly printed, as governor-general of Canada 1888-93 (2 boxes).
Liverpool RO (920 Der 16). Deposited by the 18th Earl of Derby 1980. NRA 20761.

See also *Cabinet Ministers.*

STANMORE, Baron, see Hamilton-Gordon AC.

STAPLETON-COTTON, see Cotton.

[316] STEPHEN, Sir Alfred (1802-1894)
Administrator of New South Wales 1872, lieutenant-governor 1875-91.

Corresp with his family, governors of New South Wales and others 1826-93 (1 vol); diaries 1837-9, 1844, 1849-53, 1862, 1871, 1873-88 (22 vols); reminiscences, literary extracts, notes and verses (4 vols, 88pp).
Mitchell Library, Sydney (ML MSS 777). Bequeathed 1963 by his granddaughter Ruth Bedford. NRA 25898.

Letter books as a judge and as chief justice of New South Wales 1838-48 (5 vols).
Mitchell Library, Sydney (A 669-73).

Autobiography 1802-91.
Dixson Library, Sydney (MSQ 324). Bequeathed by Sir William Dixson 1952.

Letters from Sir SJ Way 1882-94 (1 bundle).
State Library of South Australia Archives Department, Adelaide (PRG 30/8). Presented among Way's papers 1944. NRA 27637.

[317] STEPHEN, George Milner (1811-1894)
Administrator of South Australia 1838.

Diaries 1838-9 (2 vols); 'Memoranda of my Administration of the Government of South Australia' 1838, and other papers 1839-94 (2 vols).
Mitchell Library, Sydney (A 1694, C 702). Acquired from EAH Stephen 1927-42.

[318] STEPHEN, Sir James (1789-1859)
Assistant under secretary for war and the colonies 1834-6, permanent under secretary 1836-48.

Letters to his son JF Stephen and others c1834-1859, and letters from Thomas Carlyle 1853-4 and Sir George Stephen 1855 (57 items); diary 1846 (1 vol).
Cambridge University Library (Add 7349, 7511). Presented by Miss DJ Stephen. NRA 28108.

Letters from Lord Glenelg 1835-6 (18 items) and from the 3rd Earl Grey 1834-53 (52 items); misc corresp c1845-53; transcripts by his daughter Caroline of letters from him to various correspondents 1807-59.

Cambridge University Library (Add 7888). Deposited by Professor GS Graham 1970.

[319] STEWART, Robert (1769-1822), styled Viscount Castlereagh 1796-1821, 2nd Marquess of Londonderry 1821
Secretary of state for war and the colonies 1805-6, 1807-9.

Corresp, memoranda, reports, etc 1805-9, mainly concerning the conduct of the war in Europe, but incl material rel to appointments of colonial governors, defence of Gibraltar, British N America and the W Indies, abolition of the slave trade, commerce between the W Indies and the United States, capture of Cape Colony and intervention in Spanish America (c1,300 items); Colonial Office secret service accounts 1805-6, 1807-9 (4 vols).
Public Record Office of Northern Ireland (D3030). Presented 1976 by the National Trust after deposit 1974-5 by Lady Mairi Bury, daughter of the 7th Marquess of Londonderry. NRA 12865.

See also *Cabinet Ministers.*

[320] STEWART, Major-General William (1769-1854)
Lieutenant-governor of New South Wales 1824-7.

Misc corresp and papers 1801-54 incl letters from Sir Ralph Darling and papers rel to his army career and his estates in Scotland 1801 and New South Wales 1827 (1 vol); additional instructions 1825, copies of his oaths on taking office 1825, legal papers 1843, 1848 (1 box).
Dixson Library, Sydney (MSQ 403-4). Bequeathed by Sir William Dixson 1952. NRA 25525.

[321] STEWART-MACKENZIE (formerly **STEWART**), **James Alexander** (1784-1843)
Governor of Ceylon 1837-41; high commissioner for the Ionian Islands 1840-3.

Corresp and papers, India 1817-36, mainly as a commissioner of the Board of Control 1832-4; Ceylon 1836-41, incl letters from Lord John Russell, papers rel to the charter of justice 1837-9, household and personal accounts 1837-43; Ionian Islands 1840-3, incl copies of despatches and letters to the Colonial Office, corresp with Sir Richard Church and Sir Edmund Lyons, material rel to relations with the senate, public administration etc; personal, estate, political and other corresp 1794-1843, incl letters from Henry Goulburn, the 2nd Viscount Melville and Lord Sidmouth; corresp and papers rel to Ross and Cromarty affairs 1787-1847; personal and household accounts 1837-43.
Scottish Record Office (GD 46). Presented by Mr and Mrs FA Stewart-Mackenzie 1954. *List of gifts and deposits,* ii, pp26-30.

Corresp with Lord Glenelg, Lord Normanby, Lord John Russell, Sir RJ Wilmot-Horton, members of his family and others 1837-41; copies of despatches received and sent 1837-41; corresp, despatches and

papers (mainly copies) of previous governors, Ceylon 1815-37; corresp and papers rel to the Sinhalese judiciary and legislature, church affairs, appointments, his libel case against the *Ceylon Herald* etc 1837-44; addresses, memorials and other printed papers c1840-3; journal, private accounts, notes on the history etc of Ceylon 1837-41, with related papers 1815.
Department of National Archives, Colombo, Sri Lanka. Acquired in 1951 from Mr and Mrs FA Stewart-Mackenzie through the Ceylon Manuscripts Commission. NRA 28126.

[322] **STORKS, Lieutenant-General Sir Henry Knight** (1811-1874)
High commissioner for the Ionian Islands 1859-63; governor of Malta 1864-5, of Jamaica 1865-6.

Private letter book 1862-3 (1 vol); official papers, Ionian Islands 1862 (1 vol); petitions to him, Jamaica 1866 (6 vols); printed papers rel to New Zealand 1865 and Jamaica 1866 (2 vols).
National Army Museum (6807/255). Presented by the Royal United Service Institution 1968. NRA 20823.

[323] **STRACHEY, Sir Henry** (1736-1810), 1st Bt 1801
Non-permanent under secretary for home affairs 1782-3.

Corresp with and papers rel to the Clive family 1765-1807 (2 vols, 28 bundles and items); general corresp, India 1764-1804 (3 vols, 2 bundles); misc papers, mainly India, 1755-1801 (24 bundles and items).
India Office Library and Records (MSS Eur F 128/ 93-153). Purchased from the 2nd Baron Strachie 1965. NRA 8898; *HMC Sixth Report, Appendix*, pp396-9.

Corresp, instructions, etc as secretary to the commission for restoration of peace in the American colonies 1776-8 (18 items); journals 1776, 1777 (2 vols); intercepted letters from French Canadians c1776-8 (several packets); corresp and papers rel to the peace of Paris 1782-3 (18 items); letters from William Tryon, governor of New York, to Lord Dartmouth 1774-6 (33 items).
Untraced. HMC Sixth Report, Appendix, pp399-404.

Memorial from New York loyalists to the peace commissioners [1776].
New York Historical Society. Presented 1947 by an anonymous donor who had purchased it from the 2nd Baron Strachie. *HMC Sixth Report, Appendix*, pp401-2.

Copies of reports from governors and other papers rel to N American and W Indian colonies 1768-75 (2 vols); misc corresp 1776-7 (6 items).
William L Clements Library, University of Michigan, Ann Arbor. Purchased at Sotheby's 13 Nov 1922, lot 396 (property of the 1st Baron Strachie) and 3 July 1967, lot 242. NRA 24303.

Letters to him from statesmen, soldiers and others 1776-83, and a letter from him 1776 (16 items).
Library of Congress, Washington (Ac 5032A). Purchased from EC Lampson 1935. NRA 24302.

Letters mainly from Edward Bancroft, American double-agent in Paris 1782-3 (12 items).
North Yorkshire RO. Purchased 1982 from the 7th Baron Bolton among the papers of Thomas Orde, secretary to the Treasury. NRA 8638 (4/6).

Corresp with his wife while in America 1776-8, and with Patrick Tonyn and others mainly rel to his Florida plantation 1771-1802 (1 vol, c83 items); accounts rel to sales of slaves, etc 1774-1802 (several hundred pages).
Untraced. Sold at Sotheby's 17 Dec 1981, lot 83.

Letters mainly from his son Richard 1799-1809, with misc related papers (2 vols).
Somerset RO (DD/SM). Bequeathed by the 2nd Baron Strachie 1973. NRA 8898.

[324] **STUART, Lieutenant-General Sir Charles** (1753-1801)
Governor of Minorca 1798-1800.

His correspondence printed in *A prime minister and his son: from the correspondence of the 3rd Earl of Bute and of Lt-general the Hon Charles Stuart, KB*, ed Mrs E Stuart Wortley, 1925, has not been traced.

Letters from Sir JT Duckworth 1798-9 (27 items), and Lord Keith 1798-9 (4 items); letter from him to Sir William Hamilton 1799.
National Library of Scotland (MS 7199). Purchased at Sotheby's 14 Nov 1955, lot 1058.

[325] **SWAYNE, Brigadier-General Hugh** (d 1836)
Administrator of Cape Breton 1812-16.

Official corresp with Colonial Office and Audit Office 1812-13 (40pp); official letter book 1813-15 (48pp); military and naval corresp and returns 1812-15 (98pp); memorials, reports and other papers rel to civil administration of Cape Breton 1788-1815 (232pp); personal corresp 1813-17 (125pp); papers rel to the Demerara expeditions 1797-8 (35pp); financial and misc papers 1789-1819 (160pp).
Public Archives of Canada, Ottawa (MG24 A5). Deposited by him in Cox & Co's bank 1832, and presented by Lloyds Bank Ltd through Colonel CP Stacey 1955.

[326] **SWETTENHAM, Sir Frank Athelstane** (1850-1946)
Resident in Selangor 1882-9 (acting resident in Perak 1884-6); resident in Perak 1889-96; resident-general in the Federated Malay States 1896-1901, governor of the Straits Settlements 1901-4.

Journals 1874-6, 1883, mainly Selangor and Perak (13 vols); corresp and papers 1874-1903, Malaya

and Straits Settlements, incl memoranda and draft proposals for administration of the Malay states 1893-4 (*c*80 items); corresp and papers 1905-45, mainly concerning his part in the formation of the Federated Malay States (*c*60 items, etc).
National Archives of Malaysia, Petaling Jaya (SP 12). Purchased from his trustees 1948, except for seven journals deposited 1965 by the Malaysian high commissioner. National Archives of Malaysia, *Swettenham papers*, 1970.

SYDNEY, Viscount, see Townshend.

TAUNTON, Baron, see Labouchere.

[327] TENNENT, Sir James Emerson
(1804-1869), 1st Bt 1867
Lieutenant-governor of Ceylon 1847; governor of St Helena 1850 (did not proceed).

General corresp 1833-69, incl letters from John Doyle 1842-65, and Lords Fitzgerald 1841-3, Stanley 1851-3 and Torrington 1847-54 (1,432 items); corresp and papers rel to Irish politics 1830-62 (250 items); as secretary to the Board of Control 1841-5 (18 items); rel to Ceylon and St Helena 1845-53, incl corresp with Lord Grey and the Colonial Office and papers rel to the House of Commons Ceylon committee (258 items); as secretary to the Poor Law Board and Board of Trade 1852-67 (53 items); personal, family, literary and misc corresp and papers 1815-69, incl European travel journals 1825, 1840-1 (*c*325 vols and items); Irish estate and business corresp and papers 1773-1880 (8 vols, 512 items).
Public Record Office of Northern Ireland (D 2922). Deposited 1979 by Rosamond, Lady Langham, widow of his great-grandson Sir JCP Langham Bt. NRA 23442.

Drawings, water-colours and photographs for his *Ceylon: an account of the island* (1859), incl letters to him rel to Sinhalese customs, history, religion etc *c*1859 (2 vols).
Untraced. Offered for sale at Sotheby's 15 Dec 1980, lot 159.

[328] TENNYSON, Hallam (1852-1928), 2nd Baron Tennyson 1892
Governor of South Australia 1899-1902; acting governor-general of Australia 1902, governor-general 1903-4.

Corresp with British and Australian statesmen, politicians, churchmen and others 1895-1924, mainly 1899-1904 (*c*250 items); copies of secret despatches to secretaries of state for the colonies 1902-4 (1 vol); telegrams to him and drafts of telegrams from him 1902-4 (272 items); addresses to him 1899-1903 (6 vols); visitors' book 1899-1903 (1 vol); misc commissions, accounts and other papers 1899-1904 (2 files, *c*55 items); diaries 1900-3 (4 vols); photographs, press cuttings and other printed papers 1895-1912 (14 vols, *c*150 items).

National Library of Australia, Canberra (MS 479). Deposited on permanent loan by the 4th Baron Tennyson 1958. NRA 22803.

Letters from Australian governors, politicians and others 1893-1913, mainly 1901-3 (316pp); copies of despatches from Australian governors to the secretary of state for the colonies 1902-3 (62pp); misc papers, mainly printed 1902-3 (109pp).
National Library of Australia, Canberra (MS 1963). Presented by Lincoln Public Library 1967. NRA 22803.

Letters to him mainly rel to British and Australian politics 1880, 1893-1917, with draft speeches, etc 1866-1914 (1 vol).
Mitchell Library, Sydney (A 5011). Purchased from IK Fletcher, dealer 1950.

[329] THESIGER, General Frederic Augustus
(1827-1905), 2nd Baron Chelmsford 1878
Lieutenant-governor of Cape Colony 1878-9.

Letters from Sir HBE Frere 1878-9 (1 bundle); corresp with the War Office 1878-81 (2 bundles); corresp with military commanders and other papers rel to Kaffir and Zulu wars 1877-9 (18 bundles); misc corresp 1879-86 (2 bundles); copies of his letters to Frere, the Duke of Cambridge and others 1878-9 (3 vols); telegrams 1878-9 (6 vols); intelligence reports from Zulu sources 1879 (1 vol); drafts of speeches and articles, maps and misc papers (3 bundles).
National Army Museum (6807/386). Presented by the 2nd Viscount Chelmsford through the Royal United Service Institution 1968. NRA 20795.

[330] THOMPSON, General Thomas Perronet
(1783-1869)
Governor of Sierra Leone 1808-10.

Many of his papers are reported to have been destroyed by fire in 1874 at the Pantechnicon depository, London (LG Johnson, *General T Perronet Thompson*, 1957, p5).

Corresp with the Colonial Office, EH Columbine, Thomas Ludlam, William Wilberforce and others 1808-10, minutes of council 1808-9, vice-admiralty court proceedings 1808-9, and memoranda, reports, etc mainly rel to the slave trade and legal cases arising from it, the defence of Sierra Leone and the capture of Senegal 1807-10 (*c*5 bundles, *c*180 items); journal 1808; letters (some copies) to Thomas Ludlam from Zachary Macaulay and others 1804-9 (30 items); corresp, memoranda, etc rel to Sierra Leone after his departure 1810-12, 1820, 1838 (35 items); corresp, copies of despatches, etc, Persian Gulf and India 1818-21 (283 items); corresp and papers 1808, 1824-68 mainly rel to his career as a political reformer (5 bundles, 100 items); corresp and papers of his son Charles and granddaughter Edith mainly rel to their unpublished biographies of him, incl many copies of letters from him (some in his own hand) to his family and political associates 1828-69.

Brynmor Jones Library, Hull University (DTH). Presented by his great niece Mrs Isabel Hughes. NRA 10609.

Letters to him from his family, radical politicians and others 1808-55 (20 items); letters from him mainly to his family 1809-68 (144 items); misc notes and memoranda nd (7 bundles).
Brotherton Library, Leeds University (MS 277). Presented 1970 by the widow of his biographer LG Johnson. NRA 15923.

[331] **THURSTON, Sir John Bates** (1836-1897) Administrator of Fiji 1879-80, 1883-4, lieutenant-governor 1886-7; governor of Fiji and high commissioner for the Western Pacific 1887-97.

Diary and notebook rel to the cession of Fiji 1874 (1 vol); diary 1894 (1 vol); commonplace book containing essays, notes and five journals 1854-66 (1 vol).
National Library of Australia, Canberra (MS 1914). Purchased 1967 from John Millington, who obtained them from Thurston's second daughter Alys.

Journal of voyage from Fiji to the New Hebrides and back in search of voluntary emigrants 1871 (1 vol); journal of cruise to inaugurate the British protectorate over the Gilbert and Ellice Islands 1893 (1 vol).
National Archives of Fiji, Suva (L52, 56).

Letters and papers incl genealogical notes by Thurston and his sons, *c*35 letters from him to his sister Eliza West Morton, and typescript copy of a longer version (destroyed) of the journal of his voyage from Fiji 1871.
In private possession. See DA Scarr, *The majesty of colour: a life of Sir John Bates Thurston,* i, Canberra 1973.

[332] **TOWNSHEND, Thomas** (1733-1800), 1st Baron Sydney 1783, 1st Viscount Sydney 1789 Secretary of state for home affairs 1782-3, 1783-9.

The Sydney papers from Frognal, Kent, were dispersed at auction by Knight, Frank and Rutley in 1915. The present location of many is unknown.

Corresp, drafts, secret instructions, memoranda etc rel to the peace negotiations 1782-3 (51 items); other corresp and papers as home secretary rel to colonial affairs, incl letters from Sir George Yonge, Cabinet colleagues, politicians and colonial governors, 1782-9 (*c*250 items); corresp and papers of Sydney and his father rel to the W Indies, incl the St Eustatius affair 1781 and the Leeward Islands during the American war, 18th cent (*c*200 items), and rel to Treasury business, incl taxation of the American colonies *c*1763-8.
William L Clements Library, University of Michigan, Ann Arbor. Acquired from several sources 1918-34.

Political corresp 1766-99, mainly 1781-9 (214 items).
Brotherton Library, Leeds University (Townshend MSS).

Corresp and memoranda rel to trade with Newfoundland, and to Canadian and Nova Scotian affairs, incl the settlement of loyalists, 1750-98 (1 vol).
Public Archives of Canada, Ottawa (MG 23 A3). Acquired 1916.

Corresp with George III and Lord Chatham, Cabinet minutes and other papers 1765-87, mainly rel to the peace negotiations 1782-3 (41 items).
Huntington Library, San Marino, California. Purchased from Charles J Sawyer Ltd, booksellers, 1917.

See also *Cabinet Ministers.*

[333] **VAUGHAN, Lieutenant-General Sir John** (*c*1731-1795) Governor of Martinique 1794-5.

Letters, despatches and memoranda from colonial governors, military and naval officers and others, as c-in-c Leeward Islands 1780-1 (3 vols).
William L Clements Library, University of Michigan, Ann Arbor. Purchased 1927. E Vosper, 'Report on the Sir John Vaughan papers', *Bulletin of the William L Clements Library,* xix, 1929, pp5-37.

Letters from Lord George Germain, the Duke of Portland, Lord Rodney and others 1779-95, and misc military papers *c*1776-80 (*c*65 items).
British Library (Egerton MSS 2134 ff34-44, 2135-7 *passim*). Purchased 1871.

Corresp, etc rel to his military career in N America and W Indies 1775-92.
National Library of Wales (Lisburne MSS). Deposited by the 7th Earl of Lisburne 1947. Access restricted.

[334] **WALDEGRAVE, Admiral William** (1753-1825), 1st Baron Radstock 1800 Governor of Newfoundland 1797-9.

Corresp with Lord Collingwood, DR Morier, Lord Nelson, William Parry, members of his family and others, incl misc letters rel to Newfoundland 1797-9 (11 boxes); account of proceedings at Tunis 1796 (1 vol).
National Maritime Museum (MS 82/077). Deposited by Mrs OJ Diggle 1982. NRA 26356.

Account of his mission to Tunis 1796 (1 vol).
Lewis Walpole Library, Farmington, Connecticut.

[335] **WALKER, Brigadier-General Alexander** (1764-1831) Governor of St Helena 1822-8.

Official and private corresp 1822-31 (4 vols); copies of official and private letters from him 1823-8 (3 vols), and of official corresp with Sir Hudson Lowe 1823-5 (4 vols); governor's minute books 1823-8 (5 vols) and order books 1823-8 (2 vols); papers rel to defence, shipping, agriculture, etc, St Helena 1807-28 (10 vols); journal of his voyage to St Helena 1823 (1 vol); journals and sketch books of his sons

1823-8 (5 vols); corresp, letter books, journals, reports, orders, etc, India c1781-c1815 (119 vols); corresp and papers following his retirement from E India Co service c1812-22 (21 vols); family, literary and estate papers 18th-19th cent (419 vols).
National Library of Scotland (MSS 13601-14193). Presented by Tods, Murray & Jamieson, WS, Edinburgh 1952.

[336] **WAY, Sir Samuel James** (1836-1916), Bt 1899
Administrator of South Australia 1877, 1878, 1883, 1889, lieutenant-governor 1891-1916.

General and personal corresp 1852-1914; corresp and papers 1889-92 as chief justice of South Australia, and rel to the Imperial Federation League and to his appointment as lieutenant-governor (43 items); corresp rel to an amendment to the Commonwealth bill 1900; letter books 1854-60, 1871-4, 1891, 1897-1916 (21 vols); papers, mainly printed, rel to his administration of government 1875-1901; corresp and papers as a solicitor c1853-87, and rel to his personal financial affairs 1862-1916; commissions, letters patent, etc 1863-1915 (94 items); diaries 1879-93, 1896-1915 (35 vols); European travel journal 1897 (1 vol); misc personal papers, press cuttings, etc 1847-1924.
State Library of South Australia Archives Department, Adelaide (PRG 30). Presented by the Public Trustee 1944. NRA 27637.

[337] **WELD, Sir Frederick Aloysius** (1823-1891)
Governor of Western Australia 1869-74, of Tasmania 1874-80, of the Straits Settlements 1880-7.

Corresp with his parents and others 1845-91, journals of his travels in New Zealand 1843-54, memoranda rel to the Maori war 1845, addresses presented to him 1866-8, pamphlets and press cuttings rel to New Zealand 1851-69 (4 vols, 1 file, 63 items).
National Archives of New Zealand, Wellington (Weld Papers). Presented by Colonel HJG Weld 1958. NRA 9927; NANZ *Cumulative list of holdings 1976*, p58; *Union catalogue of New Zealand and Pacific manuscripts in New Zealand libraries*, i, p107.

Corresp mainly with politicians and army officers, New Zealand 1846-69, and a few letters of condolence to his widow 1891 (62 items).
Alexander Turnbull Library, Wellington (qMS sequence). Mainly purchased 1970 from the estate of KA Webster. NRA 25529.

Misc corresp, pedigrees and genealogical notes 1868-85 (1 bundle); diary 1879 (1 vol).
Dorset RO (D16/F35, F35A). Deposited by Colonel HJG Weld 1956, 1981. NRA 9927.

[338] **WENTWORTH, Sir John** (1737-1820), 1st Bt 1795
Governor of New Hampshire 1766-76; lieutenant-governor of Nova Scotia 1792-1808.

Letter books, New Hampshire 1767-78 (3 vols), Nova Scotia 1792-1807 (5 vols), and as surveyor-general of the king's woods in N America 1783-1808 (1 vol).
Public Archives of Nova Scotia, Halifax (RG1, vols 49-57). NRA 27280.

Letters from secretaries of state, Nova Scotian administrators and politicians and others 1768-1801 (2 vols); letters from him to Daniel Peirce 1763-6 and John Peirce 1783-1803, and misc material rel to him (1 vol).
Public Archives of Nova Scotia, Halifax (MG1, vols 939-41). NRA 27280.

Corresp mainly rel to the defence of Nova Scotia 1791-1813 (49 items).
Edinburgh University Library (Dc.1.15).

[339] **WHITWORTH-AYLMER** (formerly AYLMER), **General Matthew** (1775-1850), 5th Baron Aylmer 1785
Governor-in-chief of British North America 1830-5.

Corresp with the Colonial Office 1830-5 (7 vols); general corresp, British N America 1830-7 (3 vols); addresses to him and replies 1831-5 (1 vol).
Public Record Office (CO 387). Presented to the Colonial Office by the 11th Baron North 1897.

[340] **WILKS, Colonel Mark** (c1760-1831)
Governor of St Helena 1812-16.

Corresp and papers 1782-1826, mainly rel to his career in India (1 vol); corresp and papers 1813-23, mainly St Helena, incl notes of conversations with Napoleon Bonaparte 1816 (2 vols); commission as colonel 1814.
British Library (Add MSS 57313-15, Add Ch 75747). Presented by Brigadier HR Norman 1971.

[341] **WILLIAMS, William** (d 1837)
Governor-in-chief of Rupert's Land 1818-21; governor of the southern department of Rupert's Land 1821-6.

Letters to him, with related material, 1818-26 (1 vol); copies of letters to him 1818-20 (3 vols) and from him 1818-26 (10 vols).
Provincial Archives of Manitoba, Winnipeg (HBCA D1-2). Deposited among the Hudson's Bay Co archives 1971.

[342] **WILLIAMS, General Sir William Fenwick** (1800-1883), Bt 1856
Administrator of Canada 1860-1; lieutenant-governor of Nova Scotia 1865-7; governor of Gibraltar 1870-6.

Official and personal corresp with the Duke of Cambridge, Edward Cardwell, Lords Carnarvon and Clarendon, Sir CH Doyle, Sir EH Head, Lord Monck and others 1854-67, family corresp 1807-16, journal letters to his sister during his journey from Ceylon to England 1834, letters of

appointment and addresses to him 1855-80 (c444 items).
New Brunswick Museum, Saint John (Sir Fenwick Williams Papers, shelf 55). Presented by Mrs D Warner 1955.

Misc letters, despatches and commissions 1825-70 (1 vol).
Royal Artillery Institution (MD/917). Access by written application. NRA 22969.

[343] **WILMOT-HORTON** (formerly **WILMOT**), **Sir Robert John** (1784-1841), 3rd Bt 1834
Under secretary for war and the colonies 1821-8; governor of Ceylon 1831-7.

Corresp, mainly as under secretary, with politicians, colonial governors and officials, soldiers, diplomats, writers and others 1806-37 (163 vols); corresp and papers, arranged by subject, rel to slavery in the W Indies, emigration to Australia and British N America, and other colonial affairs c1821-8, to Ceylon, incl church matters and government relations with the press c1830-40, to British and Irish politics, and to personal, business and estate matters 1807-37 (525 vols, bundles and items); family corresp and deeds 1600-1800, incl many letters to him (10,000 items); misc papers c1820-40.
Derby Central Library (Catton Collection). Deposited by DWH Neilson. NRA 27876.

Letters as governor of Ceylon from Lords Glenelg, Ripon and Stanley 1832-7; précis of despatches received from 1836; papers rel to administration of Ceylon 1833.
Department of National Archives, Colombo, Sri Lanka. Among papers of JA Stewart-Mackenzie acquired through the Ceylon Manuscripts Commission in 1951. NRA 28126.

Letters from Lord Bathurst mainly rel to Canada and the W Indies 1824-7 (1 vol).
Mitchell Library, Sydney (A 73). Acquired as part of the DS Mitchell collection.

[344] **WILSON, General Sir Robert Thomas** (1777-1849)
Governor of Gibraltar 1843-8.

Letters to him mainly from statesmen 1803-48 (1 vol); general corresp 1828-46, incl letters from the 1st Earl of Durham and the 1st Baron Howden (1 vol); journals, memoranda and other papers, Cape Colony, St Helena, etc 1805-6 (2 vols).
British Library (Add MSS 30096-7, 30112, 30115). Purchased from his son-in-law the Revd Herbert Randolph 1876.

See also *Diplomats*.

[345] **WINDHAM, William** (1750-1810)
Secretary of state for war and the colonies 1806-7.

Misc letters, memoranda, etc to and from Lord Grenville and others rel to colonial affairs 1806-7.

British Library (Add MSS 37845-7 *passim*, 37883-6 *passim*). Purchased 1909.

See also *Cabinet Ministers.*

[346] **WINGATE, General Sir Francis Reginald** (1861-1953), 1st Bt 1920
Governor-general of the Sudan 1899-1916; high commissioner for Egypt 1917-19.

Corresp and press cuttings, Egypt and Sudan 1884-c1931 (c123 vols and boxes); corresp and papers arranged by subject rel to Abyssinia, Arabia, Darfur, Egypt, Somaliland, Sudan, etc mainly 1902-20 (c35 boxes); personal corresp and papers 1878-1951 (13 boxes); diaries 1881-6, 1897-9 (10 vols); papers of and rel to Josef Ohrwalder (3 boxes), Sir HML Rundle (1 box) and Sir RC von Slatin (4 boxes); notes on the history of Sudan and the Egyptian army, printed papers, etc c1877-c1934.
Sudan Archive, Durham University Library (Wingate Papers). Presented by Sir REL Wingate Bt 1958.
Guide to manuscripts and documents in the British Isles relating to the Middle East and North Africa, ed N Matthews and MD Wainwright, 1980, pp252-6.

Arabic letters, telegrams and addresses to him 1889-1925 (c80 items); captured Mahdist letter books and other papers.
Sudan Archive, Durham University Library (Arabic Manuscripts Collection). Presented by Sir REL Wingate Bt 1958, and purchased 1960-1. NRA 11057.

Corresp, reports, maps, etc 1884-1955, mainly as director of military intelligence, Egypt 1890-1 (345 items).
William R Perkins Library, Duke University, Durham, N Carolina. Presented 1970.

[347] **WINSLOW, Edward** (1746-1815)
Administrator of New Brunswick 1787-8, 1808.

Corresp, diaries, accounts and papers 1775-1815, rel to American loyalist claims 1788, the Maine-New Brunswick boundary commission 1796-8, his judicial career 1796-1808, etc, with family papers 1731-1877 and a collection of material 1695-1835 rel to New Brunswick boundaries (35 vols).
Harriet Irving Library, University of New Brunswick, Fredericton (MG H2). Transferred from the New Brunswick Museum, in which they had been deposited by EP Winslow and Mrs E Winslow-Spragge.

[348] **WODEHOUSE, John** (1826-1902), 3rd Baron Wodehouse 1846, 1st Earl of Kimberley 1866
Secretary of state for the colonies 1870-4, 1880-2.

Corresp and papers as governor of the Hudson's Bay Co 1866-8 (3 bundles); corresp rel to colonial affairs with statesmen, governors and others incl Sir Henry Barkly, Lord Dufferin, WE Gladstone, RGW Herbert, Lord Normanby, Sir HGR Robinson and Queen Victoria 1870-4, 1880-2 (144

bundles); memoranda, confidential print and other papers rel to colonial affairs 1867-86, incl Canadian confederation and defence 1867-73 and the Zulu and Boer wars 1878-81 (39 bundles); political journal 1868-73 (1 vol); appointments diaries 1871-2 (2 vols); patronage book 1880-2.
In family possession. Not open for research. NRA 1274. A microfilm of the Canadian papers is in the Public Archives of Canada, Ottawa (MG27 IA4).

See also *Cabinet Ministers.*

[349] **WODEHOUSE, Sir Philip Edmond**
(1811-1887)
Superintendent of British Honduras 1851-4; governor of British Guiana 1854-7, of Cape Colony 1861-70.

Many of his papers are reported to have been destroyed in 1915, after the death of his only son (CW de Kiewiet, *British colonial policy and the South African republics 1848-1872*, 1929, pp xi-xii).

Corresp mainly with secretaries of state for the colonies and with his son 1861-9 (1 vol).
Foreign and Commonwealth Office Library (Acc 13015).

Corresp with secretaries of state for India, viceroys and others, and misc papers, as governor of Bombay 1872-7 (3 boxes).
India Office Library and Records (MSS Eur D 726). Presented by his daughter-in-law 1915. NRA 27461.

[350] **WOLSELEY, Field-Marshal Garnet Joseph** (1833-1913), Baron Wolseley 1882, 1st Viscount Wolseley 1885
Administrator of the Gold Coast 1873-4, of Natal 1875; high commissioner for Cyprus 1878-9, for Natal and the Transvaal 1879-80.

Many of his papers were presented to the Royal United Service Institution after being used by Sir GCA Arthur and Sir FB Maurice, *Life of Lord Wolseley*, 1924. Some of these were deposited in the War Office in 1940 (transferred to the Public Record Office 1964) and *c*1946, and others in the Cameronians Museum. In 1970 the remaining papers at the Royal United Service Institution were presented to Hove Central Library, which already held other papers bequeathed by his daughter, Viscountess Wolseley.

Letters mainly to him from members of the royal family, statesmen, soldiers, colonial governors and others 1834-1921 (*c*3,500 items); congratulatory letters and telegrams 1894-5 (223 items); letters to him from his wife 1867-1911 (*c*1,670 items); letters from him to his wife 1870-1912 (*c*2,230 items) and to other members of his family 1852-87 (242 items); private letter books 1878-90 (4 vols); memoranda books 1875, 1882-8 (4 vols); corresp and papers mainly rel to his literary works *c*1880-*c*1905, but incl his personal diary and misc papers 1875 (*c*200 vols, boxes and bundles); commissions, letters of appointment, passports, etc mainly 1854-1906 (83

items); scrapbooks rel to his career compiled by his daughter (33 vols).
Hove Central Library. NRA 10471.

Journals 1873-5, 1878-80, 1884-5 (6 vols); copies of telegrams, Sudan 1884-5 (5 vols); cavalry brigade order book, China 1860; incomplete MS of his *Narrative of the war with China in 1860* (1862).
Public Record Office (WO 147)

Printed official reports and memoranda *c*1874-90, annotated by him, with a few manuscript letters and reports (50 vols).
Ministry of Defence (Whitehall) Library (Class W).

Copies of semi-official corresp, Cyprus 1878-9 (1 vol).
British Library (Add MS 41324). Purchased at Sotheby's 14 June 1926, lot 448.

Copies of letters and despatches to FA Stanley and others 1879-80 (1 vol).
Killie Campbell Africana Library, Durban (KCM 53176). NRA 28622.

Personal diaries 1877-83, 1885, 1900-6 (15 vols).
Cameronians (Scottish Rifles) Museum, Hamilton, Lanarkshire.

Index to his autograph collection 1883 (1 vol).
In private possession. NRA 10471.

[351] **WOOD, Field-Marshal Sir Henry Evelyn**
(1838-1919)
Administrator of Natal and commissioner for the settlement of the Transvaal 1881.

Corresp mainly with statesmen, soldiers and colonial administrators, telegrams, reports, orders, etc, Gold Coast 1873-4 (3 vols), Natal and Transvaal 1878-81 (13 vols), Egypt 1882-4 (5 vols), S Africa 1899-1902 (2 vols); personal corresp 1874-1913 (2 vols); letters and telegrams from him and others to his wife 1880-2 (1 vol); misc corresp and papers 1882,1902, nd (2 vols).
Natal Archives Depot, Pietermaritzburg (A 598). NRA 17233.

Letters to him from statesmen, soldiers, colonial governors and others, with a few copies of replies, and other papers, 1852-1919 (*c*700 items); family corresp *c*1887-1919 (176 items); commissions, etc 1855-91 (21 items); sketches, photographs, press cuttings and other printed papers *c*1857-1919 (2 vols, *c*240 items).
Killie Campbell Africana Library, Durban (Wood Papers). Purchased from JL Blair 1982. NRA 28127.

Corresp with Lord Roberts and others rel to the Zulu war, the Transvaal, Egypt, etc 1848-1919 (232 items).
William R Perkins Library, Duke University, Durham, N Carolina. Mainly acquired 1962.

Letters from Lord Kitchener, Sudan 1897-8 (1 vol).
National Army Museum (6807-234). Presented by the Royal United Service Institution 1968. NRA 18641.

WYNN-CARRINGTON, see Carington.

[352] **YOUNG, Sir John** (1807-1876), 2nd Bt
1848, Baron Lisgar 1870
High commissioner for the Ionian Islands 1855-9;
governor of New South Wales 1860-7;
administrator of Canada 1868-9, governor-general
1869-72.

Letter book 1856-7, incl copies of letters to John
Ball, Sir GF Bowen and Henry Labouchere.
Untraced. Typescript copies are in private
possession. NRA 23439.

Letters to him from the 5th Duke of Newcastle and
others, with misc papers, 1849-65 (16 items).
Nottingham University Library (Ne C11052-67).
Deposited among the Newcastle papers 1955. NRA
7411.

[353] **YOUNG, Sir William** (1749-1815), 2nd Bt
1788
Governor of Tobago 1807-15.

Corresp and papers mainly rel to his family estates
in the W Indies 1768-1835, incl observations by
him on his father's conduct and claims 1793, letters
from him 1809-11, and memoranda of his
transactions with W India merchants 1810 (10 vols).
Rhodes House Library, Oxford (MSS W.Ind.t.1).
Presented by Clara, Lady Young.

Abstract of British W Indian trade and navigation
1770-1805 (1 vol); account by him of Tobago 1809
(1 vol); *Almanack for the Island of Tobago for 1810*
containing notes and drawings by him (1 vol);
privately printed journal of his Italian tour 1772,
with manuscript notes and drawings (1 vol); essay
on Paestum 1773 (1 vol); drawings of
Buckinghamshire militia uniforms 1793 (1 vol).
British Library (Stowe MSS 488, 791, 921-3, 1022).
Purchased 1849 from the 2nd Duke of
Buckingham, to whose grandfather they had been
presented by Young.

His sketch maps and water-colours mainly of
Tobago, some with explanatory notes, late 18th-
early 19th cent (1 vol, 13 items).
Institute of Commonwealth Studies, London (WIC
103). Acquired with the West India Committee's
library 1976; formerly in the possession of his
great-grandson Sir CL Ottley. NRA 18538.

Index of institutions

The references are to entry numbers

TAUNTON
Somerset Record Office 125, 173, 187, 323

TORONTO
Archives of Ontario 178, 292, 298, 306
Metropolitan Toronto Library 8, 100, 284, 298

TULSA, Oklahoma
Thomas Gilcrease Institute of American History
and Art 199

VANCOUVER
University of British Columbia Library 267

VICTORIA
Provincial Archives of British Columbia 91, 101,
158, 244

WARWICK
Warwick County Record Office 300

WASHINGTON, DC
Howard University Library 67
Library of Congress 54, 72, 217, 323

WELLINGTON
Alexander Turnbull Library 28, 45, 146, 171, 197,
337
National Archives of New Zealand 39, 45, 116, 337

WIGAN
Wigan Record Office 127

WILLIAMSBURG, Virginia
Swem Library, College of William and Mary 247

WINCHESTER
Hampshire Record Office 266

WINNIPEG
Provincial Archives of Manitoba 79, 91, 121, 227,
307, 341

WORCESTER
Hereford and Worcester Record Office 265

Printed in the UK for HMSO by Hobbs the Printers of Southampton
(1247) Dd738624 C17 9/86 G381